CONFRONTING GLOBAL WARMING

Energy Production and Alternative Energy

CONFRONTING GLOBAL WARMING

Energy Production and Alternative Energy

Debra A. Miller

Michael E. Mann
Consulting Editor

GREENHAVEN PRESS
A part of Gale, Cengage Learning

GALE
CENGAGE Learning

Detroit • New York • San Francisco • ~~New Haven,~~ Conn. • Waterville, Maine • London

GALE
CENGAGE Learning

Christine Nasso, *Publisher*
Elizabeth Des Chenes, *Managing Editor*

© 2011 Greenhaven Press, a part of Gale, Cengage Learning

For more information, contact:

Greenhaven Press
27500 Drake Rd.
Farmington Hills, MI 48331-3535
Or you can visit our Internet site at
gale.cengage.com.

For product information and technology assistance, contact us at
Gale Customer Support, 1-800-877-4253.
For permission to use material from this text or product, submit all requests online at
www.cengage.com/permissions.
Further permissions questions can be e-mailed to
permissionrequest@cengage.com

Every effort is made to ensure that Greenhaven Press accurately reflects the original intent of the authors. Every effort has been made to trace the owners of copyrighted material.

Cover image copyright © taraki, 2010, used under license from Shutterstock.com; image copyright © JinYoung Lee, 2010, used under license from Shutterstock.com; leaf icon © iStockPhoto.com/domin_domin.

**LIBRARY OF CONGRESS
CATALOGING-IN-PUBLICATION DATA**

Miller, Debra A.
    Energy production and alternative energy / Debra A. Miller.
        p. cm. -- (Confronting global warming)
    Includes bibliographical references and index.
    ISBN 978-0-7377-5106-2 (hardcover)
    1. Renewable energy sources--Juvenile literature. 2. Electric power production--Juvenile literature. I. Title.
    TJ808.2.M548 2010
    333.79'4--dc22
                                    2010024976

Printed in the United States of America
1 2 3 4 5 6 7 14 13 12 11 10

Contents

Preface

> *"The warnings about global warming*
> *have been extremely clear for a long*
> *time. We are facing a global climate*
> *crisis. It is deepening. We are entering*
> *a period of consequences."*
>   *Al Gore*

Still hotly debated by some, human-induced global warming is now accepted in the scientific community. Earth's average yearly temperature is getting steadily warmer; sea levels are rising due to melting ice caps; and the resulting impact on ocean life, wildlife, and human life is already evident. The human-induced buildup of greenhouse gases in the atmosphere poses serious and diverse threats to life on earth. As scientists work to develop accurate models to predict the future impact of global warming, researchers, policy makers, and industry leaders are coming to terms with what can be done today to halt and reverse the human contributions to global climate change.

Each volume in the Confronting Global Warming series examines the current and impending challenges the planet faces because of global warming. Several titles focus on a particular aspect of life—such as weather, farming, health, or nature and wildlife—that has been altered by climate change. Consulting the works of leading experts in the field, Confronting Global Warming authors present the current status of those aspects as they have been affected by global warming, highlight key future challenges, examine potential solutions for dealing with the results of climate change, and address the pros and cons of imminent changes and challenges. Other volumes in the series—such as those dedicated to the role of government, the role of industry, and the role of the individual—address the impact various facets of society can have on climate change. The result is a series that provides students and general-interest readers with a solid understanding of the worldwide ramifications of climate change and what can be done to help humanity adapt to changing conditions and mitigate damage.

Each volume includes:

- A descriptive **table of contents** listing subtopics, charts, graphs, maps, and sidebars included in each chapter
- Full-color **charts, graphs, and maps** to illustrate key points, concepts, and theories
- Full-color **photos** that enhance textual material
- **Sidebars** that provide explanations of technical concepts or statistical information, present case studies to illustrate the international impact of global warming, or offer excerpts from primary and secondary documents
- **Pulled quotes** containing key points and statistical figures
- A **glossary** providing users with definitions of important terms
- An annotated **bibliography** of additional books, periodicals, and Web sites for further research
- A detailed **subject index** to allow users to quickly find the information they need

The Confronting Global Warming series provides students and general-interest readers with the information they need to understand the complex issue of climate change. Titles in the series offer users a well-rounded view of global warming, presented in an engaging format. Confronting Global Warming not only provides context for how society has dealt with climate change thus far but also encapsulates debates about how it will confront issues related to climate in the future.

Foreword

E arth's climate is a complex system of interacting natural components. These components include the atmosphere, the ocean, and the continental ice sheets. Living things on earth—or, the biosphere—also constitute an important component of the climate system.

Natural Factors Cause Some of Earth's Warming and Cooling

Numerous factors influence Earth's climate system, some of them natural. For example, the slow drift of continents that takes place over millions of years, a process known as plate tectonics, influences the composition of the atmosphere through its impact on volcanic activity and surface erosion. Another significant factor involves naturally occurring gases in the atmosphere, known as greenhouse gases, which have a warming influence on Earth's surface. Scientists have known about this warming effect for nearly two centuries: These gases absorb outgoing heat energy and direct it back toward the surface. In the absence of this natural greenhouse effect, Earth would be a frozen, and most likely lifeless, planet.

Another natural factor affecting Earth's climate—this one measured on timescales of several millennia—involves cyclical variations in the geometry of Earth's orbit around the sun. These variations alter the distribution of solar radiation over the surface of Earth and are responsible for the coming and going of the ice ages every 100,000 years or so. In addition, small variations in the brightness of the sun drive minor changes in Earth's surface temperature over decades and centuries. Explosive volcanic activity, such as the Mount Pinatubo eruption in the Philippines in 1991, also affects Earth's climate. These eruptions inject highly reflective particles called aerosol into the upper part of the atmosphere, known as the stratosphere, where they can reside for a year or longer. These particles reflect some of the incoming sunlight back into space and cool Earth's surface for years at a time.

Human Progress Puts Pressure on Natural Climate Patterns

Since the dawn of the industrial revolution some two centuries ago, however, humans have become the principal drivers of climate change. The burning of fossil fuels—such as oil, coal, and natural gas—has led to an increase in atmospheric levels of carbon dioxide, a powerful greenhouse gas. And farming practices have led to increased atmospheric levels of methane, another potent greenhouse gas. If humanity continues such activities at the current rate through the end of this century, the concentrations of greenhouse gases in the atmosphere will be higher than they have been for tens of millions of years. It is the unprecedented rate at which we are amplifying the greenhouse effect, warming Earth's surface, and modifying our climate that causes scientists so much concern.

The Role of Scientists in Climate Observation and Projection

Scientists study Earth's climate not just from observation but also from a theoretical perspective. Modern-day climate models successfully reproduce the key features of Earth's climate, including the variations in wind patterns around the globe, the major ocean current systems such as the Gulf Stream, and the seasonal changes in temperature and rainfall associated with Earth's annual revolution around the sun. The models also reproduce some of the more complex natural oscillations of the climate system. Just as the atmosphere displays random day-to-day variability that we term "weather," the climate system produces its own random variations, on timescales of years. One important example is the phenomenon called El Niño, a periodic warming of the eastern tropical Pacific Ocean surface that influences seasonal patterns of temperature and rainfall around the globe. The ability to use models to reproduce the climate's complicated natural oscillatory behavior gives scientists increased confidence that these models are up to the task of mimicking the climate system's response to human impacts.

To that end, scientists have subjected climate models to a number of rigorous tests of their reliability. James Hansen of the NASA Goddard Institute for Space Studies performed a famous experiment back in 1988, when he subjected a climate model (one relatively primitive by modern standards) to possible future fossil fuel emissions scenarios. For the scenario that most closely matches actual emissions since then, the model's predicted course of global temperature increase shows an uncanny correspondence to the actual increase in temperature over the intervening two decades. When Mount Pinatubo erupted in the Philippines in 1991, Hansen performed another famous experiment. Before the volcanic aerosol had an opportunity to influence the climate (it takes several months to spread globally throughout the atmosphere), he took the same climate model and subjected it to the estimated atmospheric aerosol distribution. Over the next two years, actual global average surface temperatures proceeded to cool a little less than 1°C (1.8°F), just as Hansen's model predicted they would.

Given that there is good reason to trust the models, scientists can use them to answer important questions about climate change. One such question weighs the human factors against the natural factors to determine responsibility for the dramatic changes currently taking place in our climate. When driven by natural factors alone, climate models do not reproduce the observed warming of the past century. Only when these models are also driven by human factors—primarily, the increase in greenhouse gas concentrations—do they reproduce the observed warming. Of course, the models are not used just to look at the past. To make projections of future climate change, climate scientists consider various possible scenarios or pathways of future human activity. The earth has warmed roughly 1°C since preindustrial times. In the "business as usual" scenario, where we continue the current course of burning fossil fuel through the twenty-first century, models predict an additional warming anywhere from roughly 2°C to 5°C (3.6°F to 9°F). The models also show that even if we were to stop fossil fuel burning today, we are probably committed to as much as 0.6°C additional warming because of the inertia of the climate system. This inertia ensures warming for a century to come, simply due to our greenhouse gas emissions thus far. This committed warming introduces a profound procrastination penalty for not taking immediate action. If we are to avert an additional warming of 1°C, which would bring the net warming to 2°C—often considered an appropriate threshold for defining dangerous human impact on our climate—we have to act almost immediately.

Long-Term Warming May Bring About Extreme Changes Worldwide

In the "business as usual" emissions scenario, climate change will have an array of substantial impacts on our society and the environment by the end of this century. Patterns of rainfall and drought are projected to shift in such a way that some regions currently stressed for water resources, such as the desert southwest of the United States and the Middle East, are likely to become drier. More intense rainfall events in other regions, such as Europe and the midwestern United States, could lead to increased flooding. Heat waves like the one in Europe in summer 2003, which killed more than thirty thousand people, are projected to become far more common. Atlantic hurricanes are likely to reach greater intensities, potentially doing far more damage to coastal infrastructure.

Furthermore, regions such as the Arctic are expected to warm faster than the rest of the globe. Disappearing Arctic sea ice already threatens wildlife, including polar bears and walruses. Given another 2°C warming (3.6°F), a substantial portion of the Greenland ice sheet is likely to melt. This event, combined with other factors, could lead to more than 1 meter (about 3 feet) of sea-level rise by the end of the century. Such a rise in sea level would threaten many American East Coast and Gulf Coast cities, as well as low-lying coastal regions and islands around the world. Food production in tropical regions, already insufficient to meet the needs of some populations, will probably decrease with future warming. The incidence of infectious disease is expected to increase in higher elevations and in latitudes with warming temperatures. In short, the impacts of future climate change are likely to have a devastating impact on society and our environment in the absence of intervention.

Strategies for Confronting Climate Change

Options for dealing with the threats of climate change include both adaptation to inevitable changes and mitigation, or lessening, of those changes that we can still affect. One possible adaptation would be to adjust our agricultural practices to the changing regional patterns of temperature and rainfall. Another would be to build coastal defenses against the inundation from sea-level rise. Only mitigation, however, can prevent the most threatening changes. One means of mitigation that has been given much recent attention is geoengineering. This method involves perturbing the climate system in such a way as to partly or fully offset the warming impact of rising greenhouse gas concentrations. One geoengineering approach involves periodically shooting aerosol particles, similar to ones produced by volcanic eruptions, into the stratosphere—essentially emulating the cooling impact of a major volcanic eruption on an ongoing basis. As with nearly all geoengineering proposals, there are potential perils with this scheme, including an increased tendency for continental drought and the acceleration of stratospheric ozone depletion.

The only foolproof strategy for climate change mitigation is the decrease of greenhouse gas emissions. If we are to avert a dangerous 2°C increase relative to preindustrial times, we will probably need to bring greenhouse gas emissions to a peak within the coming years and reduce them well below current levels within the coming decades. Any strategy for such a reduction of emissions must be international and multipronged, involving greater conservation of energy resources; a shift toward alternative, carbon-free sources of energy; and a coordinated set of governmental policies that encourage responsible corporate and individual practices. Some contrarian voices argue that we cannot afford to take such steps. Actually, given the procrastination penalty of not acting on the climate change problem, what we truly cannot afford is to delay action.

Evidently, the problem of climate change crosses multiple disciplinary boundaries and involves the physical, biological, and social sciences. As an issue facing all of civilization, climate change demands political, economic, and ethical considerations. With the Confronting Global Warming series, Greenhaven Press addresses all of these considerations in an accessible format. In ten thorough volumes, the series covers the full range of climate change impacts (water and ice; extreme weather; population, resources, and conflict; nature and wildlife; farming and food supply; health and disease) and the various essential components of any solution to the climate change problem (energy production and alternative energy; the role of government; the role of industry; and the role of the individual). It is my hope and expectation that this series will become a useful resource for anyone who is curious about not only the nature of the problem but also about what we can do to solve it.

Michael E. Mann

Michael E. Mann is a professor in the Department of Meteorology at Penn State University and director of the Penn State Earth

System Science Center. In 2002 he was selected as one of the fifty leading visionaries in science and technology by Scientific American. *He was a lead author for the "Observed Climate Variability and Change" chapter of the Intergovernmental Panel on Climate Change (IPCC) Third Scientific Assessment Report, and in 2007 he shared the Nobel Peace Prize with other IPCC authors. He is the author of more than 120 peer-reviewed publications, and he recently coauthored the book* Dire Predictions: Understanding Global Warming *with colleague Lee Kump. Mann is also a co-founder and avid contributor to the award-winning science Web site RealClimate.org.*

CHAPTER 1

Energy and Global Warming: An Introduction

The phenomenon of global warming, also called climate change, is much more than just another environmental issue. Rather, as most scientists acknowledge, global warming is basically an energy crisis, caused by the world's two-hundred-year-long dependence on fossil fuels such as petroleum, coal, and natural gas. As professor and author Michael T. Klare writes:

> Global warming is . . . an energy problem, first and foremost. Almost 90 percent of the world's energy is supplied through the combustion of fossil fuels, and every time we burn these fuels to make energy we release carbon dioxide into the atmosphere; carbon dioxide, in turn, is the principal component of the "greenhouse gases" (GHGs) that are responsible for warming the planet. Energy use and climate change are two sides of the same coin.[1]

According to most energy experts, therefore, the solution to global warming is nothing less than a global energy revolution that replaces human dependence on fossil fuels with new, non-polluting, renewable energy sources. This transition will probably require both regulation of greenhouse gas emissions and large-scale, fundamental changes in energy policies that could affect all aspects of human civilization.

The Fossil Fuel Era

The global dependence on fossil fuels developed during the Industrial Revolution, two centuries of economic and social development that transformed the way modern humans work and live. Most historians agree that the Industrial Revolution began in the early 1700s in Great Britain when machinery began to replace manual labor and animal power, and fossil fuels replaced wind, water, and wood as sources of energy. Before this period in history, humans manufactured goods by hand or using very simple machines, and most people worked at their homes, which were typically located in rural areas. With the invention of new industrial machines, production of goods was made easier and faster, and work moved out of the home and into urban areas. For example, the invention of a number of new textile machines led to the creation of the first large textile factories, expanding textile production greatly. Similar advancements in iron making techniques increased Britain's production of iron, a material used to make many of the new machines and a variety of other products.

Perhaps the most important machine invented during this initial phase of the Industrial Revolution, however, was the steam engine—a machine that burned coal to create steam energy used to power various types of machinery. The first steam engine was invented in 1698, but it wasn't until the design was improved by Scottish inventor James Watt in the late 1700s that the steam engine became a source of mechanical and transportation power critical to the spread of the Industrial Revolution. Soon, coal-fueled steam engines were used to drive factory machinery and to power farm tractors, as well as for transportation of goods via steamships and steam-powered locomotives. By the 1800s, powered by steam and coal, the industrialization process had spread throughout Europe and to North America, and was on its way to the rest of the world.

In the late 1800s and 1900s, the Industrial Revolution continued with the dawning of the oil era. This period was the re-

Henry Ford's mass-produced Model T car made internal combustion vehicles standard in the United States and around the world. SSPL/Getty Images.

sult of two key events—the drilling of the first oil wells in the United States and the invention and development of the internal combustion engine. The oil era was born in 1859 in the United States, when a former railroad worker named Edwin L. Drake used a steam engine to drill a well to underground oil and pump it to the surface, launching a new industry—the refining of oil for kerosene fuel for use in lamps and lighting. Later in the 1800s many people turned to natural gas as a fuel for lighting. Early in the next century, American entrepreneur Henry Ford founded an automobile company to manufacture automobiles with internal combustion engines that could run on gasoline, a product created during the refining of oil. In 1908 Ford launched the mass-produced Model T car, an affordable vehicle that soon made the internal-combustion vehicle the standard car design in the United States and around the world. By the 1950s oil had re-placed coal as the primary fuel for transportation. Soon, almost all forms of transportation—cars, trucks, buses, trains, ships, and airplanes—were fueled by oil or its by-products (diesel and gaso-line). Around the same time, coal-produced electricity and the incandescent light bulb replaced kerosene and gas lamps in the United States. As decades passed, the demand for oil, coal, and natural gas grew steadily in other countries as well, and fossil fu-els quickly became the dominant source of energy in the United States and in most countries around the world.

The discoveries and inventions of the Industrial Revolution created a world dangerously dependent on fossil fuels. Today, most of the developed world relies on cheap oil (along with coal and natural gas) to power the world economy and to provide the goods, amenities, and multiple modes of transportation that have become synonymous with modern lifestyles. As Steve Con-ner, the science editor for the British newspaper the *Independent* explains:

> Crude oil has been critical for economic development and the smooth functioning of almost every aspect of society. Agricul-ture and food production is heavily dependent on oil for fuel and fertilisers. In the US, for instance, it takes the direct and indirect use of about six barrels of oil to raise one beef steer. It is the basis of most transport systems. Oil is also crucial to the drugs and chemicals industries and is a strategic asset for the military.[2]

This fossil fuel dependence, however, is producing greenhouse gas emissions (GHGs) such as carbon dioxide, methane, and nitrous oxide that scientists say are trapping the sun's rays and warming the global climate in potentially catastrophic ways.

According to the International Panel on Climate Change (IPCC), carbon dioxide emissions from fossil fuel use from 1970 to 2004 accounted for almost 57 percent of all global [greenhouse gas] emissions, with the remainder resulting mostly from deforestation and agriculture.

The Global Warming Problem

Although some scientists and critics still dispute that human-caused GHGs are causing climate change, the majority of scientists and climate experts assert that global warming is a serious problem that could have devastating consequences unless action is taken to reduce fossil fuel emissions. In 2007, for example, the Nobel Prize–winning Intergovernmental Panel on Climate Change (IPCC), a scientific body charged by the United Nations with summarizing the best climate science, concludes that evidence of the warming of our climate is "unequivocal."[3] The 2007 IPCC report also found that global GHG emissions have dramatically increased since preindustrial times—including an increase of 70 percent between 1970 and 2004—and the report concludes that this increase is "very likely"[4] due to human activities such as the burning of fossil fuels. According to the IPCC, carbon dioxide emissions from fossil fuel use from 1970 to 2004 accounted for almost 57 percent of all global GHG emissions, with the remainder resulting mostly from deforestation and agriculture.

The consequences of global warming that are already being felt, according to IPCC, include more frequent heat waves, heavy precipitation, and increasing average sea levels. In addition, more areas seem to be affected by drought, and the number of extremely cold days has decreased. Mountain glaciers and snow cover have also decreased in both the northern and southern hemispheres, and Arctic sea ice is rapidly disappearing. Unless humans make changes to reduce GHG emissions, this warming process is expected to continue, bringing possibly irreversible consequences for the planet. According to the IPCC, this could mean the loss of animal and plant species, as well as large-scale degradation of fisheries, water resources, and terrestrial eco-systems, which could threaten human health, jeopardize global food production, result in water shortages, and create staggering economic and social upheaval around the world.

Solutions to Energy-Related Global Warming

Addressing global warming, however, is a highly complex and daunting endeavor. Many climate experts have urged the world to stabilize GHG concentrations in the atmosphere around 450 to 550 parts per million (ppm)—that is, no more than 450 to 550 units of greenhouse gases for every million units of air in the earth's atmosphere. This approach, experts say, could keep average global temperatures at no more than 3.6° Fahrenheit (2° Celsius) above preindustrial levels, which could avoid some of the worst, irreversible consequences of climate change. Such a goal is just slightly higher than current levels, which are about 380 ppm, and according to the IPCC would require drastic global GHG emission reductions—20 percent to 40 percent by 2020 and 50 percent to 80 percent over the next century.

Recently, however, some scientists have argued that new evidence of climate impacts, such as the surprisingly rapid loss of Arctic ice, mean that earlier projections may have seriously underestimated the amount of emission reductions needed to prevent catastrophic environmental damage. NASA scientist James Hansen, for example, maintains the melting of Arctic ice may be a tipping point that could spark massive permafrost melt-

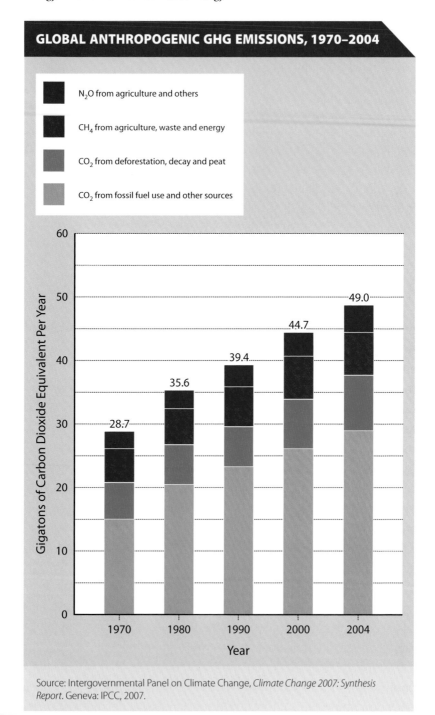

GLOBAL ANTHROPOGENIC GHG EMISSIONS, 1970–2004

Legend:
- N_2O from agriculture and others
- CH_4 from agriculture, waste and energy
- CO_2 from deforestation, decay and peat
- CO_2 from fossil fuel use and other sources

Y-axis: Gigatons of Carbon Dioxide Equivalent Per Year

X-axis: Year

Values: 28.7 (1970), 35.6 (1980), 39.4 (1990), 44.7 (2000), 49.0 (2004)

Source: Intergovernmental Panel on Climate Change, *Climate Change 2007: Synthesis Report*. Geneva: IPCC, 2007.

ing and other events that could release huge amounts of GHGs and produce accelerated climate warming. Such events—caused when rising temperatures change the environment in ways that create even more warming—are examples of feedback loops, situations in which one condition creates other conditions that reinforce the first. To ensure the return of this Arctic ice, Hansen and his colleagues have suggested a GHG target of 300 to 325 ppm—a goal far below the current level that would require substantially higher emissions reductions in the very near future. As Hansen has explained, "We either begin to roll back not only the emissions [of CO_2] but also the absolute amount in the atmosphere, or else we're going to get big impacts. . . . We should set a target of CO_2 that's low enough to avoid the point of no return."[5]

Accomplishing such ambitious goals will not be easy. The majority of proposed solutions fall into two categories: reducing fossil fuel consumption, and substituting alternative, non–GHG-emitting energy sources for fossil fuels. To date, global efforts to reduce emissions have focused on reducing consumption of fossil fuels through carbon caps. The Kyoto Protocol, a 1997 international treaty, required signatory industrialized countries to reduce greenhouse gas emissions to a level about 5 percent below 1990 levels by 2012 through the use of international carbon caps—a system that sets an overall limit on the amount of allowable carbon emissions and allows countries that cannot meet emissions reduction targets to buy carbon credits from countries that are exceeding emissions reduction goals. Many countries have enacted nationwide carbon cap programs as well. An alternative idea promoted by many energy experts, called a carbon tax, would simply tax all fossil fuels and allow those costs to be passed along to the rest of the economy, in order to reduce fossil fuel usage by making it more expensive.

The second major way to reduce emissions is to switch from fossil fuels to low- or zero-emission energy options. Various energy experts champion a variety of low-emission strategies that

A Global Warming Emergency?

If humans do not act quickly to reduce global warming emissions, the Intergovernmental Panel on Climate Change (IPCC), an international scientific body, predicts devastating consequences. According to the IPCC's 2007 report, within just a few decades, up to 30 percent of plant and animal species may go extinct, and hundreds of millions of people around the world may face severe weather such as floods and intense storms, as well as water shortages and severe heat waves. British economist Nicholas Stern has estimated that these weather impacts of global warming could also seriously damage the world economy, potentially even reducing global economic output, expressed as gross national product (GNP), by 20 percent.

The extent of global warming remains controversial, but recent data about the effects of global warming suggest that the impact of global warming may be even worse than these 2007 IPCC projections. In October 2009, for example, the U.S. National Snow and Ice Data Center announced that the past five years have seen the five lowest levels of summer Arctic sea ice since the start of satellite record-keeping in 1979. These reports of rapid Arctic ice melting suggest that Arctic sea ice may completely disappear far earlier than the IPCC's worst-case scenario predictions of the latter part of this century, perhaps within the next five years. The absence of Arctic ice could, in turn, speed up other warming effects, creating a series of feedback loops that will be impossible to control. In fact, some scientists have warned that if immediate action is not taken to cut emissions, there is a real possibility of runaway global warming that humans can no longer mitigate.

could help to slowly wean the United States and the world from dirty fossil fuels. These bridge strategies might include increased use of lower-emitting natural gas and nuclear power, the development of technologies to make coal less polluting, and the possible deployment of a new fuel—methane hydrates, a type of frozen methane found in deposits around the world.

Because no one energy source at this point appears to provide the perfect substitute for cheap fossil fuels, some experts think that employing multiple strategies could be the most effective and realistic path, at least in the near term. Researchers Stephen Pacala and Robert Socolow at Princeton University, for example, have suggested a list of many different "stabilization wedges," which together could hold emissions at approximately current levels for the next fifty years and allow the world to stabilize GHGs at about 500 ppm. The wedges could include, for example, improvements in energy efficiency and vehicle fuel economy; a greater reliance on less-polluting fossil fuel energy sources such as natural gas and nuclear power; carbon sequestration (capturing carbon dioxide emitted from fossil fuels and storing it underground); and increases in technologies such as solar, wind, geothermal, and biofuels. Such a multifaceted approach is appealing because it promises to control GHG emissions using today's knowledge and technologies.

A more ambitious idea, geoengineering, is also beginning to attract the attention of some climate experts. This field involves human attempts to alter the climate by using large-scale technologies that would manipulate major environmental systems on the earth, such as the ocean, clouds, and solar radiation.

Ultimately, however, most climate experts agree that a determined effort is needed as soon as possible to create a clean energy future through major investments in environmentally friendly, renewable technologies—solar, wind, geothermal, hydropower, biofuels, hydrogen, and lithium-ion batteries. Advancement of these technologies could solve global warming by transforming energy usage around the world. At present, however, this energy revolution has only just begun, and the challenges ahead are daunting.

Notes

1. Michael T. Klare, "Global Warming: It's About Energy," *Foreign Policy in Focus*, February 15, 2007. www.fpif.org.

2. Steve Conner, "Warning: Oil Supplies Are Running Out Fast," *Independent*, August 3, 2009. www.independent.co.uk.
3. Intergovernmental Panel on Climate Change, "Climate Change 2007: Synthesis Report, Summary for Policymakers," November 2007, p. 2. www.ipcc.ch.
4. Intergovernmental Panel on Climate Change, "Climate Change 2007: Synthesis Report, Summary for Policymakers," p. 5.
5. Quoted in David Spratt, "What's Up with Emissions Reductions of 25–40% by 2020?" *Climate Code Red*, March 7, 2009. http://climatecodered.blogspot.com.

CHAPTER 2

The World's Reliance on Fossil Fuels: Current Energy Usage

The burning of fossil fuels such as coal, petroleum, and natural gas have provided the world with the power needed for economic growth, paving the way for prosperity in many nations. Indeed, the modern world, with all its conveniences and products, literally runs on cheap fossil fuels. According to the U.S. Energy Information Administration (EIA), a government agency that provides official statistics about energy and the environment, the world currently consumes 85.64 million barrels of crude oil each day—roughly equivalent to every person on the planet using a little more than a half gallon (2 liters) of oil a day. Two thirds of the world's oil supply is used for transportation, with the remaining third used for various other purposes, such as heating; electricity generation; road surfacing; and as an essential ingredient for the manufacture of plastics, lubricants, fertilizers, pesticides, and countless other goods and necessities. Other fossil fuels—coal and natural gas—are used primarily for electricity generation and home heating. This reliance on fossil fuels is responsible for the majority of worldwide greenhouse gas (GHG) emissions, and global fossil fuel usage continues to increase each year, posing the threat of even greater global warming in the future.

Fossil Fuels and Carbon Emissions

Of the three fossil fuels, coal produces the most GHGs because of its high carbon content; when burned, coal releases large amounts of carbon dioxide. In addition, the coal mining process produces methane, a greenhouse gas that climate experts say is 25 times more potent in causing climate warming than carbon dioxide. According to the Center for Biological Diversity, an environmental group, coal is the main source of fuel for producing electricity throughout the world, accounting for 83 percent of greenhouse gas emissions in the U.S. electric power sector.

Oil currently produces about three fourths as much carbon dioxide as coal, but because oil is the main fuel used for transportation, a high-usage sector, it is also a leading GHG producer both globally and in the United States. In addition, large amounts of GHGs are released during the oil production and refining process. Because the oil that is easy to find is being depleted, oil companies are now turning to deposits that are more difficult and expensive to develop—so-called nonconventional sources such as oil extracted from oil shale and tar sands—and environmentalists say developing these sources will send considerably more carbon dioxide into the atmosphere.

The Marathon Oil Corporation's Garyville Refinery stands in Garyville, Louisiana. Patrick Semansky/Bloomberg via Getty Images.

The third major fossil fuel, natural gas, emits about half as much carbon dioxide as coal does when burned, but gas is still a major contributor to global warming. Because it is considered the cleanest of all the fossil fuels, energy experts predict that usage of natural gas will only grow in the future. To transport natural gas, producers supercool the gas and convert it to a liquid called liquified natural gas, or LNG—a process that critics say could further add to GHG emissions. As the Center for Biological Diversity explains,

> The production of liquified natural gas, or LNG . . . does extreme damage to our climate. Because of the tremendous energy required to liquefy, transport, and "regassify" LNG, LNG processing from just one plant can generate more than 24 million tons of greenhouse gases per year, equal to the annual greenhouse gas pollution from about 4.4 million cars; researchers at Carnegie Mellon University have concluded that LNG can actually produce almost as much greenhouse gas pollution as coal.[1]

Scientists conclude, therefore, that all fossil fuels pose a serious threat to the global climate.

Countries Responsible for Carbon Emissions

Developed countries that were the main participants in the Industrial Revolution have used large amounts of fossil fuel energy over the last century and are responsible for most of the GHGs that have already been released into the atmosphere. The United States, for example, is home to only about 5 percent of the world population but consistently uses about 25 percent of the world's energy. Per capita (that is, per person) the United States uses twice as much energy as other industrialized nations such as France, Germany, Japan, Italy, or the United Kingdom.

Not surprisingly, the United States is historically the world's largest contributor to global warming. According to a recent study by the environmental group Greenpeace USA, from 1960 to 2005, the United States emitted 213,608 million tons (193,785 million metric tons) of carbon dioxide, or 26 percent of total global GHG emissions. No other country even came close to the amount of U.S. emissions during this period. In fact, Greenpeace claims that the combined historic emissions of just seven states— Texas, California, Illinois, New York, Indiana, Pennsylvania, and Ohio—totaled 96,517 million tons (87,560 million metric tons) of carbon dioxide, more than any other country in the world. The group's report concludes, "The U.S. not only far exceeded every other country in the world in total cumulative carbon dioxide emissions since 1960, but also exceeded almost every other nation in per capita emissions as well."[2]

Newly developing countries, however, are fast becoming big carbon emitters. As of 2006, for example, China overtook the United States as the world's biggest emitter of GHGs. In that year China produced 6,200 million tons (5,624.64 million metric tons) of carbon dioxide, compared to the United States, which produced 5,800 million tons (5,261.76 million metric tons). Although China's per capita annual emissions (4.58 tons or 4.15 metric tons per person) still rank far below those of the United States (19.78 tons or 17.94 metric tons per person), China's rapid economic development promises to increase its per capita emissions in the future as well. China, like many other developing nations, wants to expand its economy by using the cheapest fuels available, and despite the threat of global warming, the most economical fuels continue to be fossil fuels. In fact, China is heavily reliant on coal, the dirtiest type of fossil fuel. According to the Pew Center on Global Climate Change, "coal accounts for about 65% of China's energy consumption,"[3] and this dependence on coal has caused China's GHG emissions to grow by about 80 percent since 1990.

The United States and China are followed in total carbon emissions by: Russia (1704 million tons, 1545.84 million metric tons), India (1293 million tons, 1173 million metric tons), Japan

(1247 million tons, 1131.26 million metric tons), Germany (858 million tons, 778.36 million metric tons), Canada (614 million tons, 557.01 million metric tons), the United Kingdom (586 million tons, 531.61 million metric tons), South Korea (515 million tons, 467.2 million metric tons), Iran (471 million tons, 427.29 million metric tons), Italy (468 million tons, 424.56 million metric tons), South Africa (444 million tons, 402.79 million metric tons), Mexico (436 million tons, 395.53 million metric tons), Saudi Arabia (424 million tons, 384.65 million metric tons), France (418 million tons, 379.20 million metric tons), Australia (417 million tons, 378.3 million metric tons), Brazil (417 million tons, 378.3 million metric tons), Spain (373 million tons, 338.38 million metric tons), Ukraine (329 million tons, 298.46 million metric tons), and Poland (303 million tons, 274.88 million metric tons). The overall picture of global energy usage and emissions is one of developed countries and major emerging economy nations using the most energy and producing most of today's global GHG emissions. The developed world is still ahead in per capita GHG emissions, but rapidly developing nations are leading in the growth rate of emissions. These differing contributions to climate change pose great challenges to the global effort to cap emissions.

U.S. Energy Usage

The United States, as the world's largest energy user, illustrates the close linkage between economic development, the burning of fossil fuels, and GHG emissions. For the first half of the nation's history, wood served as the primary source of energy in America. By the late 1800s coal became the replacement for wood, and by the mid-1900s the United States turned to oil and natural gas, as well as coal power. In the 1970s the nation developed a non–fossil fuel form of energy—nuclear power. But it was fossil fuels that provided the bulk of the energy that allowed the United States to grow into an economic powerhouse and a world superpower.

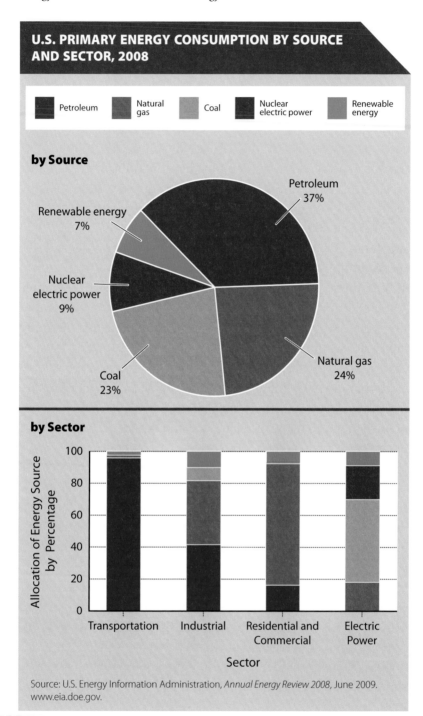

U.S. PRIMARY ENERGY CONSUMPTION BY SOURCE AND SECTOR, 2008

Petroleum   Natural gas   Coal   Nuclear electric power   Renewable energy

by Source

Petroleum
37%

Renewable energy
7%

Nuclear
electric power
9%

Coal
23%

Natural gas
24%

by Sector

Allocation of Energy Source by Percentage

100
80
60
40
20
0

Transportation   Industrial   Residential and Commercial   Electric Power

Sector

Source: U.S. Energy Information Administration, *Annual Energy Review 2008*, June 2009. www.eia.doe.gov.

Today, in the United States, 84 percent of the nation's energy comes from fossil fuels. According to the EIA, 37 percent of the energy Americans use comes from petroleum; 23 percent is provided by coal; and 24 percent is from natural gas. Nuclear power and renewable energy resources (mostly hydroelectric power) supply a relatively small portion of U.S. total energy usage, about 9 percent and 7 percent, respectively. Oil is the main source of fuel for U.S. transportation needs, while coal is the primary source of electric power generation, and natural gas is typically used for home heating. Until the late 1950s, the United States produced enough oil and coal to be self-sufficient in energy, but the depletion of U.S. oil supplies beginning in the 1970s, together with steadily increasing consumption, has caused the nation to import more and more of its oil from other countries. As of 2008 imported energy accounted for 26 percent of all energy consumed in this country.

The United States is a highly industrialized country, so the industrial sector uses the most energy—about one third (31 percent) of all the nation's energy usage. Businesses use this energy to generate steam or hot water and as part of the manufacturing process—for example, to refine petroleum, dry automobile paint, or cook packaged foods. A few industries stand out as very energy-intensive. As the EIA explains, "The petroleum refining industry is the largest industrial consumer of energy, followed closely by the chemical industry."[4]

Transportation is the U.S. sector that uses the second-largest amount of energy (28 percent)—in the form of gasoline, diesel, and jet fuel for personal automobiles, mass transit (buses, subways, trains, airplanes), and the transportation of goods (trucks, freight trains, seaway shipping). According to the EIA, there were 249 million cars, buses, and trucks in the United States in 2007—almost one vehicle for each U.S. resident, and the vast majority of transportation energy is used to fuel these personal vehicles.

Another 22 percent of U.S. energy is used in homes, largely for space heating, lighting, and water heating. Natural gas is the energy source most widely used in residences, followed by electricity, heating oil, and propane. Commercial buildings—such as shopping malls, office buildings, banks, schools, hospitals, and hotels—account for the balance of U.S. energy usage (about 19 percent), mostly for heating and lighting.

Growing Energy Demands and Emissions

Despite growing awareness of the threat of global warming, the worldwide demand for fossil fuels continues to increase year after year. According to the EIA's 2009 International Energy Outlook, an annual government report of projected energy usage, "World . . . energy consumption is projected to increase by 44 percent from 2006 to 2030."[5] The report projects that the energy demand in OECD countries—that is, the 30 developed countries that make up the international body called Organisation for Economic Co-operation and Development—will increase in the years leading up to 2030 by around 15 percent.

China is expected to produce the most greenhouse gas emissions between now and 2030.

At the same time, a number of developing countries, such as China and India, are just beginning a period of rapid industrialization and growth that is causing a marked increase in their demand for energy. According to the EIA, these less developed countries could increase their demand for energy by 73 percent over the next couple of decades. Of all the non-OECD countries, China and India are the fastest-growing developing economies, and together they currently use about 19 percent of the world's energy resources. By 2020, however, the EIA projects that the two nations will consume almost a third of world energy supplies (or about 28 percent). In contrast, the United States is projected to reduce its energy consumption over the same period, from about 21 percent to about 17 percent.

Global Warming and Peak Oil

Some climate scientists have suggested that the world might avoid some of the worst impacts of global warming because of peak oil. Peak oil theory holds that humans may have already (or will soon) reach the peak, or maximum, level of global petroleum production, and that future oil production will rapidly decline from that point onward. According to the global peak oil theory, remaining oil reserves may be far lower than most producers have publicly acknowledged, and producers are already having difficulties keeping up with growing worldwide demand. This, according to those who agree with the theory of peak oil, is the reason behind rising fuel prices, and the problem could worsen in the future as countries such as China and India require ever-larger amounts of fossil fuels for their rapidly developing economies.

While some commentators worry about peak oil sparking international conflicts or causing economic destabilization, a few commentators have projected a possible positive impact—less global warming. NASA scientist James Hansen and his colleague Pushker A. Kharecha, for example, in a 2007 article titled "Implications of 'Peak Oil' for Atmospheric CO_2 and Climate," assert that if oil production peaks within the next few decades and limits oil consumption, carbon emissions levels could be reduced, slowing climate change. Kharecha and Hansen's positive scenario depends on certain other energy choices, however, at least some of which might be very unrealistic. For example, their projection assumes that nonconventional oil sources will not be developed; that coal-powered energy plants will be phased out (in the developed world by 2012); and that deforestation will soon be arrested. The conclusion many experts have drawn, therefore, is that peak oil alone is not going to save us from global warming, although it provides yet another good reason to move away from fossil fuels as quickly as possible.

Developing countries whose demand for fossil fuel energy is increasing are expected to produce the most GHG emissions in coming years. As the EIA's 2009 International Energy Outlook explains, "In 2006, non-OECD energy-related emissions of carbon dioxide exceeded OECD emissions by 14 percent. In 2030, energy-related carbon dioxide emissions from the non-OECD countries are projected to exceed those from the OECD countries by 77 percent."[6] Of all the non-OECD developing nations, China is expected to produce the most GHG emissions between now and 2030. EIA projects that China's emissions will average 2.8 percent annually, due largely to the country's continued heavy reliance on fossil fuels, especially coal. In fact, according to EIA predictions, China will account for the bulk (74 percent) of the world's coal-related carbon emissions in future years. Altogether, experts say these trends will likely cause global GHG emissions to increase dramatically by 2030, bringing even more serious climate change—unless dramatic mitigation efforts are made.

Notes

1. Center for Biological Diversity, "Energy and Global Warming." www.biological diversity.org.
2. Greenpeace USA, "America's Share of the Climate Crisis: A State-by-State Carbon Footprint," May 2009. www.greenpeace.org.
3. Pew Center on Global Climate Change, "Climate Change Mitigation Measures in the People's Republic of China," April 2007. www.pewclimate.org.
4. Energy Information Administration, "Use of Energy in the United States Explained," July 13, 2009. http://tonto.eia.doe.gov.
5. U.S. Energy Information Administration (EIA), "Highlights," in *International Energy Outlook 2009*, Report no. DOE/EIA-0484, May 27, 2009. www.eia.doe.gov.
6. U.S. Energy Information Administration (EIA), "Energy-Related Carbon Dioxide Emissions," in *International Energy Outlook 2009*, Report no. DOE/EIA-0484, May 27, 2009. www.eia.doe.gov

Cutting Fossil Fuel Emissions

If projections about future increases in fossil fuel usage and greenhouse gas (GHG) emissions come true, scientists say that the result will be catastrophic climate changes that could change life on Earth dramatically, possibly even causing uncontrollable global warming that could lead to human extinction. According to climate experts, however, it is still possible for humans to mitigate the most dire effects of global warming. The 2007 International Panel on Climate Change (IPCC) report, for example, concluded that catastrophic global warming can be avoided if the world takes immediate and decisive action to stabilize and then reduce greenhouse gas emissions. The IPCC noted that a variety of methods could be used to achieve this goal, including international or nationwide carbon caps or taxes, regulating emissions from industry and transportation, making improvements in energy efficiency, and encouraging lifestyle changes to reduce individual carbon footprints.

The 1997 Kyoto Protocol

Recognizing the impending threat of global warming, nations of the world came together in 1997 in Kyoto, Japan, to negotiate an international agreement called the Kyoto Protocol, aimed at reducing global GHG emissions. The Kyoto agreement went into effect in 2005 and was formally approved by 172 countries. In essence, Kyoto required industrialized countries to reduce their greenhouse gas emissions to a level of 5.2 percent below 1990 levels by 2012 by using an international carbon cap system. Under Kyoto's system—called cap and trade—emission goals were set for each country, and countries that cannot cut their emissions can purchase or trade for credits from countries that are exceeding reduction goals. According to projections, the industrialized nations covered by the Kyoto treaty are on course to meet or exceed the goal of cutting emissions by 5.2 percent by 2012. Although this success is partially attributable to the economic collapse of the Soviet Union, which forcibly reduced the emissions of many Communist nations, supporters say it demonstrates the value of international climate agreements.

The Kyoto effort was flawed from the start, however, because neither the United States nor China—two of the world's biggest emitters—was covered by the treaty. The U.S. Senate declared its opposition in the 1997 Byrd-Hagel Resolution, claiming that the treaty's failure to cover developing nations such as China and India placed U.S. companies at a disadvantage and would harm the U.S. economy. As a result, U.S. presidents Bill Clinton and George W. Bush never submitted the Kyoto treaty to the Senate for ratification. At the same time, China, as a developing country, was never subject to Kyoto's restrictions. Therefore, even though the 1997 treaty will likely achieve its stated goals in many countries, the Kyoto process has failed to reduce overall global GHG emissions. As Bill Chameides, former chief scientist for the environmental advocacy group Environmental Defense Fund, explains, "Kyoto cannot be counted as an enormous success. . . . The global picture is rather bleak. Since 1990 and despite the treaty, global emissions from fossil fuel use have increased by almost 37 percent."[1]

A process is now under way to negotiate a new global emissions treaty before Kyoto expires in 2012. Most recently, representatives from around the world met in Copenhagen, Denmark, in December 2009, but the outcome proved to be disappointing to many climate advocates. Instead of a conclusive treaty that would promise clear action on global warming, the Copenhagen Climate Conference resulted in the Copenhagen Accord—a non-legally-binding declaration that allows developed nations to set their own emissions reduction targets and proposes financing from the rich countries to poor ones to help the developing world undertake emissions cuts. As Fred Boltz, head of Conservation International's Copenhagen delegation, put it, "The Copenhagen Accord, while better than nothing, is not enough."[2]

The Copenhagen Accord appeared to be the best possible deal due to continuing disagreements between developed and developing nations, particularly the United States and China. The United States wants to see developing countries such as China and India commit to binding emissions reductions along with the developed world, whereas China and other developing countries believe that developed nations must make larger cuts while allowing emerging nations a chance to develop their economies. The weak Copenhagen Accord highlighted how difficult global warming is to address and stirred up doubts about whether an effective global climate agreement can ever be achieved.

Prospects for U.S. Emission Cuts

The weakness of the Copenhagen Accord may make it less likely that the United States will enact legislation to reduce global warming emissions. Two different programs have been proposed—a nationwide cap-and-trade scheme similar to the global Kyoto system and a carbon tax, an environmental tax on carbon dioxide emissions. Proponents of a carbon tax think that a tax would be cheaper and simpler to implement than a cap-and-trade program and would avoid government bureaucracy and oversight. As energy expert William Sweet points out, "Everybody is affected equally by such a tax . . . [and] the government does not have to get into the business of picking technological winners or losers."[3] Some nations, most notably Sweden and other Scandinavian countries, have implemented carbon taxes, with varying results in terms of reducing emissions.

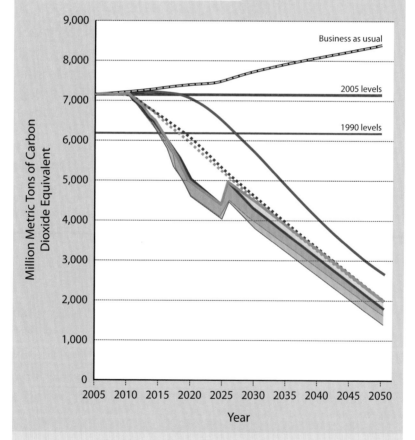

NET EMISSION REDUCTIONS UNDER CAP-AND-TRADE PROPOSALS IN THE 111TH CONGRESS, 2005–2050

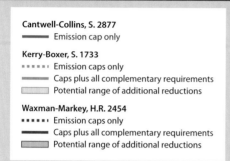

Source: John Larsen, *Emission Reductions Under Cap and Trade Proposals in the 111th Congress*, Washington, DC: World Resources Institute, 2009.

Many American policy advisors, however, worry that a carbon tax would not set a clear ceiling for the total amount of U.S. carbon emissions. As Fred Krupp, president of the advocacy group Environmental Defense Fund, explains:

> A cap puts a legal limit on pollution. A tax does not. Guessing what level of tax might drive the pollution cuts we need to avert runaway climate change is a risk we simply can't afford to take. Only a cap with strong emissions reduction targets—and clear rules for meeting them—can guarantee that we achieve the environmental goal.[4]

In addition, cap and trade is seen as more market-based because it allows companies to trade emission allowances in order to achieve maximum efficiency.

Regardless of what happens in Congress with climate legislation, the Obama administration appears ready to use the federal government's regulatory powers to reduce U.S. GHG emissions.

Cap and trade, therefore, appears to have the most supporters, including key congressional leaders and a coalition of influential environmental groups and big businesses—among them General Electric, Dow Chemical, Shell Oil, and Duke Energy. U.S. president Barack Obama also has embraced the cap-and-trade approach and has promised to press for its passage in the U.S. Congress. The administration's 2010 budget clearly states the president's emission reduction goals: "The Administration will work expeditiously with key stakeholders and Congress to develop an economy-wide emissions reduction program to reduce greenhouse gas emissions approximately 14 percent below 2005 levels by 2020, and approximately 83 percent below 2005 levels by 2050.[5]

The president lobbied to help the House of Representatives pass a climate bill—the historic American Clean Energy and Security Act—in June 2009. The House bill would institute a cap-and-trade system designed to meet the president's goals, and it also includes provisions to create clean-energy technologies, impose more efficient building standards, and require utilities to generate 15 percent of their electricity from renewable sources by 2020. Obama hoped to persuade the Senate to pass similar legislation, but cap and trade so far has failed in the Senate. After the discouraging results from Copenhagen, some legislators urged the president to postpone further work on a climate bill though others believe that a cap-and-trade bill may still be possible.

U.S. Regulatory Efforts

Regardless of what happens in Congress with climate legislation, the Obama administration appears ready to use the federal government's regulatory powers to reduce U.S. GHG emissions. The administration took a major step in this direction on December 7, 2009, when the U.S. Environmental Protection Agency (EPA) issued a final ruling that greenhouse gases endanger human health and welfare—a finding that will allow the agency to regulate the emissions of large polluters such as power plants, industrial facilities, and vehicles under the federal Clean Air Act. The EPA action was made possible by a 2007 U.S. Supreme Court decision that held that carbon dioxide and other greenhouse gases are pollutants covered by the act.

In another regulatory effort announced in May 2009, the U.S. Department of Transportation issued new Corporate Average Fuel Economy (CAFE) standards, raising the minimum miles per gallon (mpg) requirements to 30.2 mpg for cars and 24.1 mpg for light trucks by the 2011 model year. The CAFE standards will then increase by 5 percent each year until 2016, when the requirements will be 42 mpg for cars and 26 mpg for light trucks—for an overall average of 35.5 mpg. According to the EPA, the new CAFE standards will increase fuel economy by approximately 5 percent annually, reduce greenhouse gas emissions by about

950 million metric tons, save the average car buyer more than $3,000 in fuel costs, and conserve 1.8 billion barrels of oil. As EPA administrator Lisa P. Jackson explained, "We've taken the historic step of proposing the nation's first ever greenhouse gas emissions standards for vehicles, and moved substantially closer to an efficient, clean energy future."[6]

Improving Energy Efficiency

President Obama has also promoted energy efficiency as a way to reduce U.S. carbon emissions. Numerous studies have shown that making improvements in efficiency is one of the easiest ways to address the energy and climate crisis. For example, a July 2009 study conducted by the energy consulting firm McKinsey & Company estimated that "by 2020, the United States could reduce annual energy consumption by 23 percent . . . by deploying an array of . . . efficiency measures."[7] McKinsey claims that a global effort to boost efficiency could have similar results, eliminating more than 20 percent of world energy demand by 2020.

According to energy efficiency expert Amory Lovins, these gains in efficiency could be realized in many different ways. In the transportation sector alone, he says, so much energy could be saved—through better mileage, better design, and use of advanced materials—that it would be the equivalent of finding "a new Saudi Arabia under Detroit."[8] By making these and other changes, such as rewarding utility companies for saving energy and de-subsidizing the U.S. energy sector, Lovins claims that "The United States . . . could save at least half the oil and gas and three-quarters of the electricity we use."[9]

The Obama administration has already undertaken several steps to increase U.S. energy efficiency. Its economic stimulus package, the American Recovery and Reinvestment Act of 2009, included $346 million to expand and accelerate the development, deployment, and use of energy-efficient technologies in residential and commercial buildings. Also, the administration set new efficiency standards for commercial and residential appliances, such as microwaves, kitchen ranges, dishwashers, and light bulbs. According to the president, these appliance rules between 2012 and 2042 will "save consumers up to $4 billion a year, conserve enough electricity to power every home in America for 10 months, reduce emissions equal to the amount produced by 166 million cars each year, and eliminate the need for as many as 14 coal-fired power plants."[10]

Not all energy experts are convinced of the merits of energy conservation, however. In a controversial 2009 study, for example, University of Utah scientist Tim Garrett concluded that conserving energy does not really reduce energy usage, but instead encourages more economic growth and greater energy consumption. He notes that this paradoxical result occurred with coal in the mid-1800s, when coal consumption soared after improvements in steam engine efficiency. Under Garrett's model, which has been criticized by some economists, only a global economic collapse or an immediate, massive switch to noncarbon energy sources will significantly slow global warming emissions.

Geoengineering Solutions

Perhaps the most radical proposal for cutting GHG emissions is geoengineering—human manipulations of global climate mechanisms to slow global warming. Controversial Danish political scientist Bjorn Lomborg, for example, supports marine cloud whitening—pumping seawater droplets into the clouds above the ocean to make them reflect more sunlight back into space. U.S. geochemist Wallace Broecker, meanwhile, has called for research on deep ocean disposal of carbon dioxide, and atmospheric scientist Paul Crutzen has proposed injecting clouds of sulfur dioxide into the upper atmosphere to block the sun's rays.

Following page: Reforestation projects—like the one mounted on the Philippine island of Mindanao to restore mangrove trees—are among various geoengineering efforts proposed to slow global warming. Romeo Gacad/AFP/Getty Images.

Still other geoengineering proposals include massive reforestation efforts, building huge towers to suck carbon dioxide out of the air, and boosting the ocean's ability to absorb carbon dioxide by dumping tons of iron into Antarctic waters to stimulate plankton growth.

Such proposals have long been rejected by most of the world scientific community as too risky because of high costs and possible unintended environmental side effects, but geoengineering proposals are now being considered by world leaders who fear rapid global warming. President Obama's science advisor John Holdren, for example, has acknowledged that geoengineering ideas are being discussed by the administration as emergency options to address possible drastic climate change. Most climate scientists, however, still would prefer to solve the climate crisis through emissions reductions.

Individual Lifestyle Changes

Of course, residents of more developed countries can also help to cut GHG emissions by making smart lifestyle choices to reduce their individual carbon footprints—that is, the effect their lives are having on global warming. Because U.S. citizens' energy usage is more than twice that of Europeans, changes here could be significant. One of the most significant choices an individual can make is to cut back on automobile and airplane travel, because aviation and cars contribute massive amounts of GHG emissions to the atmosphere. Other actions, such as insulating homes, replacing incandescent light bulbs with more energy-efficient fluorescent or LED lights, choosing energy-efficient appliances, and turning off appliances when not in use, are also helpful. Individual action, however, is most valuable when it influences political or policy attitudes about global warming. Political activism, therefore, such as communicating concerns about global warming to legislators or joining campaigns for action on climate change, could be the most effective way for individuals to help solve climate change.

The Energy Star Program

One of the ways for U.S. consumers to help reduce greenhouse gas emissions through energy efficiency is by choosing products that feature an Energy Star label. The Energy Star was introduced by the U.S. Environmental Protection Agency (EPA) in 1992 as a voluntary labeling program designed to identify and promote energy-efficient products. The program first targeted computers and monitors, but today the Energy Star label is available on more than sixty product categories including major appliances, office equipment, lighting, and home electronics. The EPA has also extended the label to cover new homes and commercial and industrial buildings. According to the EPA, a typical American household spends $2,200 a year on energy bills, but Energy Star appliances can help to reduce that figure by more than 30 percent, or more than $700 per year, at the same time helping to cut greenhouse gas emissions.

The program works by providing a trustworthy source of information to consumers. The government tests appliances and products in order to assign a rating of how much energy each product will use. The program then provides that information to consumers and businesses to help them choose energy-efficient solutions and best management practices. According to the EPA, the Energy Star program has saved businesses, organizations, and consumers billions of dollars in energy costs and has also helped to encourage the more widespread use of technological innovations such as efficient fluorescent lighting, power management systems for office equipment, and low standby energy use.

Given the scope of the global warming challenge, however, most experts would agree that efforts to cut fossil fuel usage must be combined with plans to lower emissions and develop alternative fuels.

Notes

1. Bill Chameides, "Did the Kyoto Protocol Miss the Target?" *Green Grok*, October 12, 2009. http://nicholas.duke.edu.

2. Quoted in *Environment News Service*, "A Copenhagen Climate Accord, Not Nothing, But Not Enough," December 19, 2009. www.ens-newswire.com.

3. William Sweet, *Kicking the Carbon Habit*, New York: Columbia University Press, 2006, p. 204.

4. Quoted in *Environment 360*, "Putting a Price on Carbon: An Emissions Cap or a Tax?" May 7, 2009. http://e360.yale.edu.

5. Office of the President, "A New Era of Responsibility: Renewing America's Promise," Environmental Protection Agency, February 26, 2009, p. 100. www.gpoaccess.gov.

6. Quoted in U.S. Environmental Protection Agency, "DOT Secretary Ray LaHood and EPA Administrator Lisa P. Jackson Propose National Program to Improve Fuel Economy and Reduce Greenhouse Gases/New Interagency Program to Address Climate Change and Energy Security," September 15, 2009. http://yosemite.epa.gov.

7. McKinsey & Company, "Unlocking Energy Efficiency in the U.S. Economy," Executive Summary, July 2009. www.mckinsey.com.

8. Quoted in Alvin Powell, "Amory Lovins Talks Energy Solutions," *Harvard News Office*, 2009. www.greencampus.harvard.edu.

9. Quoted in *Environment 360*, "Amory Lovins: Energy Efficiency Is the Key," November 26, 2008. http://e360.yale.edu.

10. Barack Obama, "Remarks by the President on Energy," The White House Office of the Press Secretary, July 29, 2009. www.whitehouse.gov.

CHAPTER 4

Bridge Strategies: Low-Emission Energy Sources

Although climate experts have called for immediate and drastic cuts in fossil fuel emissions to prevent major climate change, not everyone is in agreement about how to take the next step—transitioning away from fossil fuels to clean, renewable energy sources. No one new energy source can take the place of fossil fuels, and various experts hold differing views about which strategies would be the most practical, affordable, and effective means to start the new energy revolution. Although the ultimate goal pursued by climate scientists is to implement energy technologies that produce no greenhouse gas (GHG) emissions, many experts believe lower-emission technologies that are available now, possibly including natural gas, clean coal, nuclear power, and methane energy, combined with efforts like improving energy efficiency, could bridge the gap between the most polluting types of fossil fuels—oil and coal—and a clean-energy future. These bridge strategies, supporters say, could dramatically reduce carbon emissions in the near term, giving entrepreneurs and governments the time to develop and implement renewable, nonpolluting energy sources such as solar and wind.

Natural Gas as a Transition Fuel

Natural gas—a term used for the mixture of gases (primarily methane) that have developed from decomposing plant and animal materials over millions of years—is a fossil fuel that many

MAJOR U.S. NATURAL GAS SHALE BEDS

Shale beds
Shale beds in production are labeled.

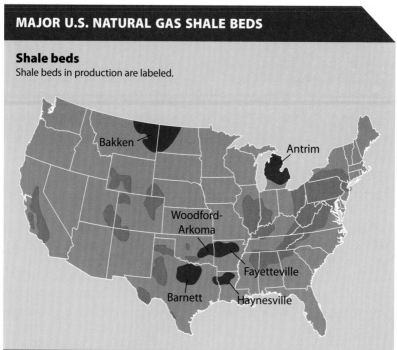

Gas reserves

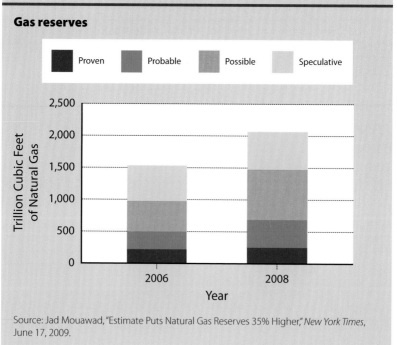

Source: Jad Mouawad, "Estimate Puts Natural Gas Reserves 35% Higher," *New York Times*, June 17, 2009.

energy experts believe could lead the transition toward cleaner energy. This is because natural gas is the least polluting type of fossil fuel, producing only about half the GHG emissions that come from the burning of coal and somewhat fewer emissions than gasoline. In addition, it is cheaper than oil and may be much more abundant, especially in the United States. Large stretches of shale in eastern states as well as in Texas, Wyoming, Arkansas, and Michigan may contain massive amounts of recoverable natural gas. In fact, the Marcellus basin, a 400-million-year-old shale formation stretching from New York to West Virginia, alone could hold up to 500 trillion cubic feet (or 14.16 trillion cubic meters) of natural gas, the equivalent of about 80 billion barrels of oil. As Tom Gjelten of National Public Radio has explained,

> Geologists have always known that shale rock, often found in combination with coal and oil deposits, holds substantial amounts of natural gas. . . . The shale gas was previously considered unreachable, but advances in drilling techniques have changed that assessment. The result is a dramatic increase in estimated natural gas reserves. The Potential Gas Committee, loosely affiliated with the Colorado School of Mines, reported in June [2009] that natural gas reserves in the United States are actually 35 percent higher than believed just two years ago, and some geologists say even that estimate is too conservative.[1]

Canada, a close U.S. ally, is also known to have vast shale reserves.

If this shale gas can be reached cheaply, substituting natural gas for oil and coal could dramatically lower U.S. GHG emissions. Perhaps the most vocal advocate of natural gas has been T. Boone Pickens, a Texas oil magnate who in 2008 and 2009 funded a $60 million publicity campaign to convince policy makers and the American public of the need to switch from petroleum to natural gas. Pickens' plan is to use wind energy to supply the nation's electricity, and then use natural gas as the primary transportation fuel, instead of diesel and gasoline. Pickens' critics, however, point out that switching cars and trucks to natural gas would require massive investments in new engines and new fueling systems. A better idea, many energy experts say, is to use natural gas, along with such renewables as solar and wind energy, to replace coal-powered electric plants, and then convert the transportation system to electricity, to power electric vehicles.

Most energy commentators are betting that natural gas will play an ever larger part in America's energy portfolio in future years.

Whatever the formula, however, most energy commentators are betting that natural gas will play an ever larger part in America's energy portfolio in future years. A recent sign of this trend was ExxonMobil's 2009 decision to buy XTO Energy Corporation, the nation's second-largest natural gas producer, for $31 million—a purchase that observers say indicates that Exxon expects tremendous future growth in natural gas.

The Clean Coal Debate

Another fuel that is abundant in the United States is coal, now the dirtiest type of fossil fuel but one that the coal industry claims can be redeemed with new technologies such as clean coal, a term often used to refer to carbon capture and sequestration (CCS)—a process of capturing the carbon dioxide produced from coal plants and storing it deep in the ocean or in geological reservoirs in the earth's upper crust. As the Web site for the American Coalition for Clean Coal Electricity (ACCCE), a group of industries involved in producing electricity from coal, states: "ACCCE supports . . . an integrated U.S. climate strategy that: Promotes rapid and widespread research, development, deployment and commercialization of innovative, advanced clean coal and other technologies—including carbon capture, transportation, safe storage, and terrestrial carbon sequestration."[2] According to some industry estimates, adding CCS technologies could reduce a coal plant's greenhouse gas emissions significantly: Luke Warren, policy manager for the World Coal Institute, an international coal advocate, projected that CCS could provide the "second-biggest [emissions] abatement potential after energy efficiency."[3]

Some energy experts agree that the prospects for CCS are encouraging. A 2007 study by the Massachusetts Institute of Technology (MIT), for example, concludes that "geological carbon sequestration is likely to be safe, effective, and competitive with many other options on an economic basis."[4]

Many environmental groups, however, say that there is no such thing as clean coal, and that the idea of CCS is nowhere close to being a commercially viable technology. As the international environmental group Greenpeace argues:

> After multi-million-dollar PR campaigns by the coal industry, many in government have become seduced by the illusion of "carbon-free coal." The industry wants Americans to believe that coal can be made safe for the environment by capturing and permanently storing the global warming pollution. This technology, Carbon, Capture and Storage (CCS) is a false hope. Despite tens of billions in public subsidies, it has never been made to work.[5]

In fact, even the supporters of CCS acknowledge that it has never been implemented in a single power plant. Clean coal critics also warn that CCS could significantly increase the price of electricity, perhaps as much as 25 percent, and that the CCS technology could not be ready in time to save the climate. The earliest deployment of CCS is not projected before 2030, and experts agree that GHG emissions must be reduced no later than 2015.

Nevertheless, the idea of clean coal has strong political support. President Obama's 2009 $787 billion economic stimulus bill included $3.4 billion to help improve CCS technology. In addition, the House climate bill provides about $60 billion to fund CCS research and development, and in February 2010, President Obama established an Interagency Task Force on CCS to develop a comprehensive federal strategy to speed the development of clean coal technologies.

Nuclear Power

Nuclear power—a currently viable source of electrical power that does not directly emit GHGs—also has many supporters. Today's nuclear power plants already provide about 20 percent of U.S. electricity by obtaining heat energy from nuclear fission, a process that involves splitting atoms of uranium rather than the burning of fossil fuels. As a Web site run by Entergy Corporation, a major U.S. nuclear power company, points out, "Nuclear power is a clean energy source that generates electricity for one in five homes and businesses in the United States without producing or emitting any greenhouse gases, including carbon dioxide."[6] In fact, even well-known environmental leaders have

A 1979 accident at the Three Mile Island Nuclear Power Plant in Pennsylvania left many Americans nervous about this mode of power generation. Bill Pierce/Time & Life Pictures/ Getty Images.

France — A Leader in Nuclear Power

One of the world's leaders in advanced nuclear technology is France, which uses nuclear power as its main source of electrical production. In fact, France now obtains more than 75 percent of its electricity from fifty-nine nuclear reactors situated throughout the country. France also exports large amounts of nuclear-produced electricity to other countries, and the French nuclear program is widely viewed as a scientific, engineering, and political success. The French greatly expanded their nuclear energy capacity in 1974, largely as a result of an Arab oil embargo that quadrupled the price of oil and shook the world economy. The embargo occurred when Arab members of the Organization of Petroleum Exporting Countries (OPEC), plus Egypt and Syria, decided to cut off shipments of oil to various countries that supported Israel during the 1973 Arab-Israeli war. As a result of this energy scare, the French government moved to build a number of new nuclear plants, largely because nuclear power would provide greater energy independence because it requires only the import of a small amount of uranium fuel.

Although the French nuclear program does have its critics, a major key to France's success with nuclear power is the French population's acceptance of nuclear energy. Many observers credit the French government with doing a good job of promoting the positive aspects of nuclear energy, especially the idea of energy independence and the fact that the nuclear program has brought jobs and prosperity to many French towns.

gone on record to support a continuation or expansion of nuclear energy as a necessary tool to reduce carbon emissions. For example, Patrick Moore, a cofounder of Greenpeace, argues in a 2006 article, "Nuclear energy may just be the energy source that can save our planet from another possible disaster: catastrophic climate change. . . . Nuclear energy is the only large-scale, cost-effective energy source that can reduce [carbon dioxide] emissions while continuing to satisfy a growing demand for power."[7] Other respected energy experts, including the Pew Center on Global Climate Change, have echoed Moore's views, insisting that nuclear power must be part of the near-term emissions mitigation equation. A number of Republican U.S. senators are also behind an expansion of nuclear power; for example, Senator Lindsey Graham (S.C.), for example, includes new subsidies for nuclear power as a key part of his efforts to draft a bipartisan climate bill in 2010.

A number of energy experts, however, challenge the idea that nuclear power is emissions-free. As environmental writer Melanie Jarman notes, "nuclear power is particularly fossil-fuel intensive [because it uses fossil fuels] for uranium mining, enrichment and transport."[8] And there is still significant opposition to nuclear fission energy because of other serious, unresolved downsides. For example, nuclear fission produces highly radioactive wastes that continue to emit lethal radiation for hundreds of years—a major problem that no country has yet remedied. In addition, after two major accidents—Three Mile Island in Pennsylvania in 1979 and Chernobyl in the former Soviet Union in 1986, there are concerns about the safety of nuclear plants. Concerns have also been raised about the environmental pollution caused by uranium mining, the radiation released during normal plant operations, and the huge amounts of water needed to cool nuclear reactors, as well as the danger that nuclear fuel could end up in the hands of terrorists or rogue nations that might use it to produce nuclear weapons. Finally, critics say nuclear plants are extremely expensive to build and cannot be built in time to have any significant effect on global warming. As Greenpeace argues in a January 2009 report,

> Nuclear power is expensive, dangerous and a threat to global security. And, when it comes to combating climate change, it cannot deliver the necessary reductions in greenhouse gas emissions in time; any emissions reductions from nuclear

power will be too little, too late and come at far too high a price.[9]

If nuclear power is to be part of the arsenal of bridge fuels, experts say the U.S. government must act quickly to expand the number of nuclear plants. A 2003 study by scientists at MIT, for example, found that nuclear power is facing stagnation and decline and requires changes in government policy and funding in order to expand. A 2009 update to the MIT report reiterates these findings, stating: "More rapid progress is needed in enabling the option of nuclear power expansion to play a role in meeting the global warming challenge. The sober warning is that if more is not done, nuclear power will diminish as a practical and timely option for deployment at a scale that would constitute a material contribution to climate change risk mitigation."[10]

Despite some previous indications to the contrary, President Obama is promoting nuclear energy as a future energy option. His 2011 budget requested $54 billion in loan guarantees for new nuclear reactors—tripling the amount previously granted by Congress, and in February 2010 the president announced that the government will offer $8.33 billion in loan guarantees for the construction and operation of two new nuclear reactors in Georgia.

Methane Energy

Another low-emission type of energy that holds promise as a bridge fuel and that exists in enormous amounts throughout the world is methane gas hydrates—a type of ice that forms when methane gas from the decomposition of organic material comes into contact with water at low temperatures and high pressures. These hydrate deposits lie in the permafrost in Arctic regions such as Alaska and beneath the ocean floor, and the U.S. Geological Survey estimates that they could contain more carbon energy than all the world's coal, oil, and nonhydrate natural gas combined. If the hydrates can be extracted in a cost-effective way, scientists say the reserves could produce vast amounts of energy with fewer carbon emissions than oil or coal. As Tim Collett, a research geologist with the U.S. Geological Survey, explains, "These gas hydrates could serve as a bridge to our energy future until cleaner fuel sources, such as hydrogen and solar energy, are more fully realized."[11]

Trapping and burning these methane hydrates for energy—which produces a relatively small amount of carbon dioxide and water vapor—may be critical for another reason as well: Large stretches of permafrost are already melting as the world climate warms, and methane, experts say, produces twenty to twenty-five times more global warming than carbon dioxide. If the methane gas is released into the atmosphere unburned, therefore, the potential greenhouse effect could be devastating to the planet. As a 2008 United Nations report explains, "Methane release due to thawing permafrost in the Arctic is a global warming wildcard. . . . The potential consequences of large amounts of methane entering the atmosphere, from thawing permafrost or destabilized ocean hydrates, would lead to abrupt changes in the climate that would likely be irreversible."[12]

Research is under way in a number of countries to assess and develop methane hydrate resources. Whether methane energy or some other transition fuel will function as the bridge that leads the world to clean energy is a question that climate experts say must be answered soon, probably within the next five to ten years, if any such reserve is to have any significant effect in slowing global warming.

Notes

1. Tom Gjelten, "Rediscovering Natural Gas by Hitting Rock Bottom," National Public Radio, September 22, 2009. www.npr.org.
2. American Coalition for Clean Coal Electricity, "Meeting the CO_2 Challenge," 2010. www.cleancoalusa.org.
3. Quoted in Toni Johnson, "Debating a 'Clean Coal' Future," Council on Foreign Relations, March 19, 2009. www.cfr.org.
4. Massachusetts Institute of Technology, "The Future of Coal: Options for a Carbon-Constrained World," 2007, p. 43. http://web.mit.edu.

5. Greenpeace, "Dirty Power Change: Coal." www.greenpeace.org.

6. Entergy Corporation, "Nuclear Energy: A Pollution Solution," 2009. http://asolutionforpollution.com.

7. Patrick Moore, "Going Nuclear: A Green Makes the Case," *Washington Post*, April 16, 2006. www.washingtonpost.com.

8. Melanie Jarman, *Climate Change*, London: Pluto Press, 2007, p. 119.

9. Greenpeace, "Nuclear Power: A Dangerous Waste of Time," January 2009. www.greenpeace.org.

10. Massachusetts Institute of Technology, "Update of the MIT 2003 Future of Nuclear Power," 2009. http://web.mit.edu.

11. Quoted in *Science Daily*, "'Ice That Burns' May Yield Clean, Sustainable Bridge to Global Energy Future," March 24, 2009. www.sciencedaily.com.

12. United Nations Environment Programme, "Methane from the Arctic: Global Warming Wildcard," UNEP Yearbook 2008, p. 46. www.unep.org.

CHAPTER 5

Developing Clean and Renewable Electrical Energy

B road agreement exists among scientists that the ideal solution to the world's energy problems and global warming is a complete switch from fossil fuels to a mix of clean, renewable, and sustainable energy sources. As the Union of Concerned Scientists, a pro-environment group of scientists, explains:

> No single solution can meet our society's future energy needs. The answer lies instead in a family of diverse energy technologies that share a common thread: they do not deplete our natural resources or destroy our environment. Renewable energy technologies tap into natural cycles and systems, turning the ever-present energy around us into usable forms. The movement of wind and water, the heat and light of the sun, heat in the ground, the carbohydrates in plants—all are natural energy sources that can supply our needs in a sustainable way. Because they are homegrown, renewables can also increase our energy security and create local jobs.[1]

Because most of the world's electricity is produced by coal, the most polluting fossil fuel, a major priority for climate researchers is finding clean ways of producing tomorrow's electricity. Most energy researchers agree that the three most viable options for this role are solar energy, wind power, and geothermal energy, followed by hydropower.

Solar Energy

Solar energy is probably the most well-known and, according to some energy experts, the most promising renewable technology. The sun, these experts say, provides ten thousand times more energy than humans need to meet 100 percent of our future energy needs. As UCS notes, "All the energy stored in Earth's reserves of coal, oil, and natural gas is matched by the energy from just 20 days of sunshine."[2] Already, solar heat collector panels installed on roofs are being used to provide hot water and produce electricity for homes and businesses, and solar concentrating systems, typically using parabolic mirrors (concave mirrors that efficiently reflect light), are creating intense heat that is used for industrial purposes or to make electricity for larger-scale applications. Another type of existing solar technology called photovoltaic (PV)—semiconductor devices often made of silicon that convert light directly into electricity—is in widespread use to power calculators and other small devices and is being developed into panels and roof tiles that can produce electricity for buildings.

To date, however, solar energy has been largely inefficient, costly, and difficult to store—problems that scientists and engineers are striving to solve. One promising new solar technology involves erecting relatively inexpensive solar power towers— huge water towers surrounded by a field of ordinary mirrors that reflect sunlight onto the tower to heat water and create steam that is used to generate electricity. Other solar researchers hope to embed textiles with tiny solar cells; these textiles could have many uses—for example, they could be woven into the structure of planes or cars or made into tents for use during disasters. Researchers also are working on storing solar energy chemically; Massachusetts Institute of Technology researchers in 2008, for example, announced that they have discovered a way to use solar energy to split water to create hydrogen, which then can be stored in hydrogen fuel cells.

In fact, some technology pundits predict that solar technologies are about to expand exponentially, due largely to the development of nanoengineered materials—that is, materials engineered at very tiny, microscopic levels—that will make solar panels lighter, more efficient, and easier to install. Nanoengineered fuel cells, for example, already have been invented, and it may be possible to create hydrogen-based fuels to power these cells and allow energy from the sun to be stored in huge quantities. As inventor and futurist Ray Kurzweil has suggested, "We are not that far away from a tipping point where energy from solar will be [economically] competitive with fossil fuels."[3]

The U.S. government apparently agrees that the future of solar is promising; the U.S. Energy Information Administration's *Annual Energy Outlook 2009* projects that the costs and efficiency of solar photovoltaics will continue to improve and that "U.S. solar photovoltaic generating capacity [will] . . . increase from 30 megawatts in 2006 to 381 megawatts in 2030."[4] In addition, the 2009 U.S. government economic stimulus package included various provisions to expand solar and other clean-energy projects, and in May 2009, President Obama committed $117.6 million of these funds for solar projects—$51.5 million of that amount for photovoltaic technology development and another $40.5 million for deployment.

Wind Power

Wind energy may rank even higher than solar in terms of its future energy potential, however. A 2008 report by Mark Z. Jacobson, a professor of civil and environmental engineering at Stanford University, concluded that wind is the most promising alternative source of energy, topping both solar and geothermal energy. Jacobson scientifically evaluated various energy solutions based on their potential for delivering energy for electricity and vehicles, their impacts on global warming, and a number of other factors. After wind, the best energy technologies, accord-

---

Following page: Wind turbines throughout the world, including these in Tarifa, Spain, are used to generate electricity. Samuel Aranda/Getty Images.

33,000 feet (10,000 meters) of the planet contains fifty thousand times more energy than all the oil and natural gas resources in the world. This heat can be used to warm homes and businesses or used as a power source for electrical power stations. Today, geothermal is already being used in twenty-four countries throughout the world, including the United States, which is reported to have more geothermal capacity than any other country. The nation currently has a capacity of about 2.5 gigawatts (GW) of geothermal electrical power, with geothermal power plants located in California, Alaska, Hawaii, Idaho, Nevada, and Utah. According to a 2008 study by the U.S. Geological Survey, however, geothermal has the potential to generate much more of the country's energy—ultimately up to 529.9 GW of electricity.

Just $3.3 billion of investment funding in research and development could make geothermal energy the cheapest energy technology in the United States, less expensive than both wind energy and fossil fuels.

Other recent scientific studies confirm this optimistic view and suggest that geothermal energy could easily and cheaply supply a substantial portion of the electricity the United States will need in the future, with minimal investment and few environmental side effects. A 2007 report by the Massachusetts Institute of Technology (MIT), for example, concluded that with reasonable investment geothermal could meet a major part of future U.S. electricity needs—up to 100 GW of cost-competitive electricity by 2050. The study also noted that geothermal energy has the advantage of producing minimal visual and other environmental impacts and virtually no GHG emissions. As Jefferson Tester, professor of chemical engineering at the MIT Laboratory for Energy and the Environment enthused, "The answer to the world's energy needs may have been under our feet all this time."[5]

An even more optimistic 2009 study by Melissa Schilling, a professor at New York University, found that geothermal has now surpassed wind as the most efficient and fastest-growing renewable energy technology. Schilling noted that the main drawbacks of hydrothermal are geographical constraints; however, hot dry rock geothermal, although more difficult and costly to develop than hydrothermal, can be developed anywhere in the country. In fact, according to Schilling, "The amount of geothermal energy is enormous; scientists estimate that United States hot dry rock resources could supply all of the United States' primary energy needs for at least 30,000 years."[6] Schilling's report concludes that just $3.3 billion of investment funding in research and development could make geothermal energy the cheapest energy technology in the United States, less expensive than both wind energy and fossil fuels. As Schilling has explained, "It is conceivable that geothermal could be cheaper than fossil fuels in just over three years—faster if fossil fuel costs go up." President Obama's economic stimulus package made the first step in this direction by including $400 million in funding for geothermal projects.

Energy from Water

Clean, renewable energy can be derived, too, from the earth's water resources. One way to harvest water energy is through hydropower (also called hydroelectric power), which uses the energy in moving streams and rivers to turn turbines to create electricity. Humans have been exploiting hydropower for thousands of years, and today it remains the largest source of renewable power in the United States and worldwide. In fact, hydropower currently provides approximately one fifth of the world's electricity, second only to fossil fuels, and world capacity is still growing steadily. The United States today produces about 95,000 megawatts (MW) of hydropower annually—about 7 percent of U.S. electricity, enough to supply about 28 million households.

In the past, hydropower facilities were often built by blocking rivers with huge dams, a technique that disrupted natural water flows and, in many cases, caused damage to fish and the surrounding environment. Hydropower, however, can be generated in other ways—for example, by diverting water from fast-flowing rivers or waterfalls through much smaller turbines, or by pumping water from low-lying regions into higher reservoirs and then releasing it downward through turbines when power is needed. Hydropower facilities can also seek certification under a voluntary program developed by the Low Impact Hydropower Institute (LIHI), a nonprofit organization that reviews projects to determine whether they meet federal and state standards to minimize harmful effects on rivers, fish, and wildlife.

The future of traditional hydropower energy may be dimming, however, because of the rapid melting of the world's glaciers as a result of global warming. Melting water from glaciers supplies much of the freshwater found in rivers and streams, so smaller glaciers will ultimately mean less moving water for hydropower facilities. For example, in Switzerland, which currently obtains 60 percent of its energy from hydropower, hydropower capacity is expected to drop to 46 percent by 2035 due to glacier losses, lack of rainfall, and increasing energy demand.

For many experts, the most exciting form of water energy today is tidal and wave energy—a process of generating electricity by capturing the hydrokinetic energy in ocean tide changes and wave action. As 70 percent of the earth's surface is covered by oceans, experts say the amount of energy that could be produced this way is vast. Hydrokinetic ocean energy is harnessed by placing and anchoring devices such as tidal barrages (or dams), fences with spinnable turnstiles, or underwater turbines in estuaries or in areas of the ocean known to have reliable offshore currents. An important advantage of this technology is that tidal and ocean currents, unlike the wind, are highly predictable. Drawbacks include possible environmental effects on fish, marine life, and nearby ecosystems. Changing tidal flows by damming an estuary could, for example, could disrupt the movement of aquatic creatures or change shoreline ecosystems. In addition, hydrokinetic

U.S. ELECTRICITY FROM RENEWABLE ENERGY BY SECTOR, 2004–2008*

Sector/ Source	2004	2005	2006	2007	2008
Biomass	53,537,453	54,276,810	54,860,621	55,538,578	55,875,118
Waste	15,420,570	15,420,393	16,098,525	16,524,554	17,086,267
Landfill Gas	5,128,425	5,142,111	5,677,040	6,157,750	6,590,366
Municipal Solid Waste Biogenic	8,150,974	8,330,471	8,477,571	8,303,838	8,459,538
Other Biomass	2,141,171	1,947,810	1,943,913	2,062,966	2,036,363
Wood and Derived Fuels	38,116,883	38,856,417	38,762,096	39,014,024	38,788,851
Geothermal	14,810,975	14,691,745	14,568,029	14,637,213	14,859,238
Hydroelectric Conventional	268,417,308	270,321,255	289,246,416	247,509,974	248,085,084
Solar/ Photovoltaic	575,155	550,294	507,706	611,793	843,054
Wind	14,143,741	17,810,549	26,589,137	34,449,927	52,025,898
TOTAL	351,484,632	357,650,653	385,771,908	352,747,486	371,688,391

* In thousand kilowatthours

Source: U.S. Energy Information Administration, "Renewable Energy Consumption and Electricity: Preliminary Statistics, 2008," July 2009. www.eia.doe.gov.

power is still in its infancy, and the costs of construction and upkeep tend to be high. In the United States, tides along the Pacific Northwest and the coast of Maine are ideal for hydrokinetic projects, but no large-scale tidal power stations have yet been built. Experts say hydrokinetic energy, however, could become very attractive. Congressman Jay Inslee of Washington state, a recognized leader in Congress on energy issues and the main sponsor of the New Apollo Energy Act, a comprehensive plan to build a clean-energy economy in America, predicts: "Wave energy will be the sleeper technology of the next two decades. There is enough potential energy in ten square miles off the coast of California to provide all that state's electricity."[7]

The key question involving all renewables, of course, is how quickly they can be developed and implemented to replace fossil fuels. Increasingly, the answer to this question is a positive one. Professor Mark Z. Jacobson and University of California-Davis researcher Mark Delucchi, for example, have prepared a plan for completely eliminating fossil fuels and powering the entire world on renewable energy by 2030. The plan calls for everything to run on electricity but would require massive investments in a variety of technologies—wind turbines, solar photovoltaic and concentrated solar systems, and geothermal, tidal, wave, and hydroelectric power sources to generate electricity—as well as new transmission lines to carry the electricity to end users. According to Jacobson and Delucchi's analysis, the savings from such a system would more than equal the costs. This vision of clean electricity, however, is only part of the solution to climate change, because the world also needs a new way to power its vehicles.

Notes

1. Union of Concerned Scientists, "Clean Energy 101," 2009. www.ucsusa.org.
2. Union of Concerned Scientists, "How Solar Energy Works," 2009. www.ucsusa.org.
3. Quoted in Robin Lloyd, "Tech Pundit Sees Bright Future for Solar Energy," FoxNews .com, March 4, 2008. www.foxnews.com.
4. U.S. Energy Information Administration, "Solar Photovoltaic and Solar Thermal Electric Technologies," in *Annual Energy Outlook 2009*, May 27, 2009. www.eia.doe.gov.

5. Quoted in Dana Childs, "MIT Report Says Geothermal Power Not to Be Ignored," Cleantech Group, January 22, 2007. http://cleantech.com.

6. Melissa A. Schilling and Melissa Esmundo, "Technology S-curves in Renewable Energy Alternatives: Analysis and Implications for Industry and Government," New York University, February 23, 2009. http://w4.stern.nyu.edu.

7. Jay Inslee and Bracken Hendricks, *Apollo's Fire: Igniting America's Clean Energy Economy*, Washington, DC: Island Press, 2008, p. 301.

CHAPTER 6

Reinventing
Transportation Energy

B ecause transportation is such a large contributor to global warming, both globally and in the United States, climate and energy experts say finding clean alternatives to gasoline is also key to replacing fossil fuels and slowing global warming. Just as there is debate and competing research about which type of alternative fuel should be developed to produce electricity, however, there is also competition among possible new transportation fuels. So far, in the United States, significant funding has been put into two transportation technologies—ethanol and hydrogen fuel cells. Many energy commentators say cars powered by electric batteries are the technology closest to mass production capability, however.

Biofuels

Biomass energy—produced from organic items such as plant and forest wastes, grass crops, human garbage, and animal wastes—is an ancient renewable fuel. Early humans created fire by burning biomass materials such as wood and animal dung, but today there are various cleaner ways to convert biomass to energy. One of the most popular methods uses heat or natural biochemical processes involving bacteria, yeasts, and enzymes to break down

Following page: An employee works in a laboratory at Imperium Grays Harbor, a biodiesel fuel plant in Aberdeen, Washington. Carlos Javier Sanchez/Bloomberg via Getty Images.

biomass materials into a liquid called ethanol, which can be used to power vehicles. In addition, biomass oils such as soybean or canola oils used in cooking, or—the newest idea—oils collected from algae, can be chemically converted into biodiesel fuel that

Brazil's Flex-Fuel Auto Industry

In March 2010 Brazil celebrated a milestone in green technology by building its ten-millionth flex-fuel vehicle—an achievement made possible by the country's robust ethanol program. The Brazilian government began promoting the production of ethanol from sugar cane, a crop traditionally grown in Brazil, in the 1970s as a result of gasoline shortages caused by an oil embargo by the Organization of Arab Petroleum Exporting Countries (OAPEC). The oil crisis clarified the dangers of many countries' dependence on foreign oil and caused Brazil in 1975 to launch a nationwide program, financed by the government, to phase out automobiles powered by gasoline in favor of cars that could run on ethanol. As a first step, the government mandated an ethanol/gasoline blend of 10 percent ethanol, but this has increased over the years to up to 25 percent. In addition, the Brazilian government subsidized ethanol production, making ethanol cheaper than gasoline. The third step taken by Brazil was to encourage local carmakers to manufacture cars and trucks that could run on ethanol. By the 1980s, one-third of Brazil's motor vehicles were running on pure ethanol. Falling gasoline prices and shortages of ethanol later in the decade posed a challenge to the program, however. The answer for Brazil was flex-fuel vehicles capable of running on any blend of gasoline and ethanol. Volkswagen produced the first such total-flex car in 2003, and soon many other car manufacturers followed this example. Today in Brazil, consumers can choose from a variety of popular flex vehicles made by such carmakers as Chevrolet, Ford, Honda, Toyota, and Nissan. By 2009, 94 percent of car and light truck sales in Brazil were flexible fuel vehicles. Many energy experts say that the United States, which also produces significant amounts of ethanol, should follow Brazil's example by encouraging production of flex vehicles and increase the number of ethanol fueling stations around the country.

can be used to fuel diesel vehicles. Similar processes can be used in landfills to turn garbage into methane gas, which then can be burned like natural gas to create electricity. Another approach is simply to mix biomass materials with coal or natural gas and burn them in existing electric power plants; this technique reduces harmful emissions because biomass emits fewer greenhouse gases (GHGs) than coal or natural gas.

Today the United States produces 12 billion gallons of ethanol a year, mainly from corn, and the ethanol is mixed with gasoline and used in many U.S. cars and trucks. The nation also supplies about 1.2 percent of the country's electricity from biomass energy. Estimates of future production are encouraging. According to a 2005 feasibility study prepared by the Oak Ridge National Laboratory for the U.S. Departments of Energy and Agriculture, biomass could supply up to 20 percent of U.S. transportation fuels and up to 15 percent of the nation's electrical energy by 2030.

The biofuel industry has strong support in the U.S. Congress. A 2007 law requires that 36 billion gallons of ethanol and other alternatives to gasoline and diesel be used in the nation's fuel mix by 2022. The government has also provided billions in subsidies and tax credits to corn-based ethanol. As the advocacy organization Environmental Working Group explains, "Corn-based ethanol . . . accounted for fully three-quarters of the tax benefits and two-thirds of all federal subsidies allotted for renewable energy sources in 2007." As of 2010, the group says "ethanol will cost taxpayers more than $5 billion a year."[1] President Barack Obama's 2009 economic stimulus package, too, included about $800 million for biomass projects. This infusion of cash has created a vital U.S. ethanol industry and spurred the development of flexible-fuel vehicles, which can run on a blend of gasoline and up to 85 percent ethanol. Each of the big U.S. automakers—GM, Ford, and Chrysler—offers flex-fuel vehicles for sale.

Biomass is controversial, however, due to claims that U.S. corn-based ethanol production requires more than a gallon of fossil fuel—to plant, fertilize, irrigate, harvest, and transport the corn—to produce one gallon of ethanol. A 2005 study by David Pimentel, a professor of ecology and agriculture at Cornell University, for example, found that corn requires 29 percent more fossil energy to grow than the fuel produced. According to some experts, therefore, biomass energy will not reduce GHG emissions. Pimentel and other critics also question the diversion of corn cropland for ethanol, which many observers believe has caused food prices to spike in the United States. An April 2009 report from the U.S. Congressional Budget Office, a federal agency that provides economic data to Congress, confirmed this claim, finding that ethanol accounted for an increase of 10 to 15 percent in food prices between April 2007 and April 2008. The report also concluded that ethanol cut gasoline usage by only 4 percent and greenhouse gas emissions by only a fraction of 1 percent.

Supporters of ethanol defend its potential. Biomass production, they argue, has changed in recent years, and advancements in ethanol conversion and greater use of cellulosic materials—such as switchgrass, fast-growing trees like poplars, and such crop wastes as corn cobs and husks—can make biofuels such as ethanol much less energy-intensive and more sustainable. Switchgrass, for example, is a type of prairie grass perennial that can be harvested each year without replanting or plowing; it also could be planted in areas in the Midwest where other agricultural crops cannot be grown. Because of these improvements, researchers Nathan Glasgow and Lena Hansen from the energy think tank Rocky Mountain Institute predict that "cost-effective and efficient ethanol production from cellulose is on the horizon . . . for the United States."[2]

Other energy experts see the long-term prospects for ethanol diminishing. Rising prices of corn, lower gasoline prices, and the economic recession that began in 2008 have forced many U.S. ethanol producers into bankruptcy. In addition, the Environmental Protection Agency (EPA) has proposed a new rule to enforce a provision in the 2007 energy bill that required any new biofuel to be at least 20 percent lower in greenhouse gas emissions than the gasoline it replaces. Under the EPA rule, new ethanol producers would have to take into account indirect carbon emissions caused by ethanol production, such as those caused by cutting down rainforests in foreign countries to create cropland. This rule, commentators say, reflects a growing realization that biofuels may not help enough with global warming, and this concern appears to be drying up financing for the ethanol industry. Nevertheless, President Obama announced in February 2010 several additional efforts to boost biofuel production, with the aim of meeting the congressional mandate of 36 billion gallons by 2022.

Hydrogen Fuel Cells

With ethanol's future uncertain, many commentators see the transportation debate evolving into a war between two other technologies—hydrogen-powered fuel cells and battery-powered electric vehicles. Some alternative fuel advocates are putting their support behind hydrogen, the most abundant element on Earth. Water, for example, is composed of hydrogen and oxygen molecules. Hydrogen can be produced from water by electrolysis, which separates the oxygen from the hydrogen. It can be used to power hydrogen fuel cells for vehicles (or to provide heat and electricity for buildings). Hydrogen fuel cells work by recombining hydrogen and oxygen—a process that produces electricity, heat, and water. Hydrogen-powered cars, therefore, could be an ideal transportation solution—nonpolluting, zero-emission vehicles that release only water, a natural and completely safe waste product. Also, fuel cells are highly efficient and powerful, and unlike typical batteries, fuel cells will never lose their charge as long as hydrogen fuel is supplied.

Hydrogen fuel cell technologies, however, must overcome many stubborn challenges before they can become a practical source of energy. Perhaps the biggest obstacle is cost; it currently takes more energy to make hydrogen than is produced, and production relies on expensive catalysts made from platinum, a

scarce metal. And like biofuels, hydrogen is currently made using fossil fuels, so it is not emissions-free. In addition, liquid hydrogen fuel is highly flammable and must be stored at very low
temperatures or under very high pressure, making transport and
storage difficult. Switching vehicles to hydrogen fuel also would
require building a whole new infrastructure similar to the chain
of gas stations that currently dot the landscape. Researchers are
hoping to find answers to these problems by searching for other
types of catalysts, studying other ways to improve production,
and developing better storage options.

Hydrogen researchers, however, have been promising breakthroughs since the 1990s with little progress to show for their
efforts. Many observers are thus coming to the conclusion that
the hydrogen fuel cell is a technology that will not be perfected
in the near future. As physicist and climate expert Joe Romm
explains, "Neither government policy nor business investment
should be based on the assumption that these technologies will
have a significant impact in the near- or medium-term."[3] The
Obama administration apparently agrees; it submitted a budget
for 2010 that sharply cut back on government support for hydrogen projects. U.S. Energy Secretary Steven Chu explained the
administration's problems with hydrogen technology:

> Right now, the way we get hydrogen primarily is from reform-
> ing [natural] gas. That's not an ideal source of hydrogen. . . .
> The other problem is, if it's for transportation, we don't have a
> good storage mechanism yet. Compressed hydrogen is the best
> mechanism [but it requires] a large volume. We haven't figured
> out how to store it with high density. What else? The fuel cells
> aren't there yet, and the distribution infrastructure isn't there
> yet. So . . . to get significant deployment, you need four signifi-
> cant technological breakthroughs. That makes it unlikely.[4]

Congress promptly reversed President Obama's decision, however, restoring more than $200 million to 190 hydrogen projects
around the country.

Electric and Hybrid Vehicles

According to many energy experts, the electric car now seems to have much more momentum than either biofuels or hydrogen, both politically and technologically. Electric cars come in three forms: (1) all-electric vehicles that plug into electrical outlets; (2) hybrid-electric vehicles, which have both a gasoline motor and an electric one; (3) and plug-in hybrids, a combination of the other two. Already, hybrid electric cars have become a hot product in many automobile showrooms. The first mass-produced hybrid was the Toyota Prius, which used a gasoline engine to provide most of the drive to the wheels, assisted by a battery-

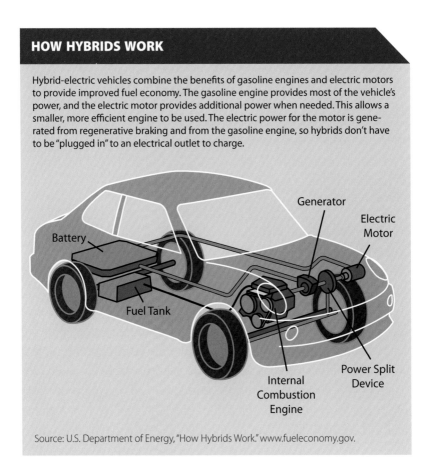

HOW HYBRIDS WORK

Hybrid-electric vehicles combine the benefits of gasoline engines and electric motors to provide improved fuel economy. The gasoline engine provides most of the vehicle's power, and the electric motor provides additional power when needed. This allows a smaller, more efficient engine to be used. The electric power for the motor is generated from regenerative braking and from the gasoline engine, so hybrids don't have to be "plugged in" to an electrical outlet to charge.

Generator

Electric Motor

Battery

Fuel Tank

Internal Combustion Engine

Power Split Device

Source: U.S. Department of Energy, "How Hybrids Work." www.fueleconomy.gov.

powered electric motor. First introduced in Japan in 1997 and worldwide in 2001, the Prius is considered by the EPA to be the most fuel-efficient car in the United States because, with its electric assist, it gets more than 50 miles per gallon of gasoline. More than a million Priuses have now been sold worldwide, more than half of them in the United States.

The newest hybrid concept is the 2011 General Motors Volt, a plug-in hybrid propelled only by its electric motor and battery; its gasoline engine merely helps when needed to turn a generator that produces electricity. Moreover, the Volt's electric battery can be plugged into an ordinary 110-volt outlet for recharging. This technology promises to give the Volt an EPA combined city/highway mileage rating of more than 100 miles per gallon, but the first 40 miles could be driven using only electric power—enough for many people to run daily errands without using any fossil fuels.

Many electric car proponents argue that it makes sense to convert to electric-powered cars first and then work to end our reliance on coal-powered electricity by moving toward natural gas and renewable sources of electricity, such as solar, wind, and geothermal.

The idea behind electric and hybrid cars is to decrease carbon emissions by reducing usage of high-emission gasoline. Hybrids, for example, stretch gasoline usage by supplementing it with electric power from a battery. The ultimate goal of many electric car advocates, however, is to mass produce an all-electric car in the near future that does not use any gasoline, making it potentially emission-free. Besides the environmental benefits, other advantages of electric cars include the fact that they run quietly, have great acceleration, and use electric fuel that costs about five times less than gasoline. Electric cars are very expensive to buy right now, but supporters say prices will drop with mass production as they are sold in larger numbers.

Yet critics charge that electric cars are not completely green because they really just substitute coal-produced electricity for gasoline. Proponents answer by citing studies showing that electric vehicles are still much cleaner than today's gas-powered cars. According to a 2006 report by the Department of Energy's Pacific Northwest National Laboratory, using today's power plants, switching from gasoline to plug-in electric vehicles would produce a reduction in total U.S. greenhouse gas emissions of 27 percent. The study also found that the existing U.S. electrical grid could power 84 percent of U.S. cars, pickup trucks, and sport-utility vehicles—a change that could displace 6.5 million barrels of oil per day, or 52 percent of the nation's oil imports. Similarly, as environmental journalist and author Jim Motavalli explains, "A study by the Los Angeles Department of Water and Power concluded that, over a 100,000-mile life cycle, a standard gas car would produce 3,000 pounds of pollutants, and an EV (electric vehicle) with power from a coal-fired power plant would produce just 100 pounds."[5] Yet another analysis by the Electric Power Research Institute (EPRI), an independent research company, found that plug-in hybrids could reduce U.S. carbon emissions significantly by 2050 if enough of them are sold. As the 2007 EPRI report stated, "Annual GHG emissions reductions were significant in every scenario combination of the study, reaching a maximum reduction of 612 million metric tons in 2050."[6]

Moreover, many electric car proponents argue that it makes sense to convert to electric-powered cars first and then work to end our reliance on coal-powered electricity by moving toward natural gas and renewable sources of electricity, such as solar, wind, and geothermal. Following this plan, supporters say, the United States could reduce its transportation emissions quickly and one day be virtually free of fossil fuels.

The key to stimulating large-scale development of electric cars, however, is producing advanced, affordable lithium-ion batteries—a new type of battery that can store twice the amount of energy density as today's standard nickel-metal-hydride batteries. Numerous countries, including the United States, are pouring billions of research dollars into this effort and hoping to emerge as the source of this critical technology. In the United States, for example, President Obama's economic stimulus plan included more than $5 billion in loans, grants, and tax credits to companies trying to develop lithium-ion batteries. Congress has also passed a $7,500 tax credit for purchases of plug-in hybrid cars, which use these batteries. Many researchers believe that success is near. As Massachusetts Institute of Technology professor Donald Sadoway explains, "We're not asking for science fiction. Most remaining problems involve engineering. So I'm optimistic that these problems that remain can be solved."[7]

No one is certain what technologies will ultimately emerge as winners in the race to develop the fuels that will wean the world from fossil fuels. Much will depend, analysts say, on the imagination of researchers, the level of private investment, and the direction and pace set by government through changes in national energy policies.

Notes

1. Environmental Working Group, "Ethanol's Federal Subsidy Grab Leaves Little for Solar, Wind and Geothermal Energy," January 2009. www.ewg.org.
2. Nathan Glasgow and Lena Hansen, "Setting the Record Straight on Ethanol," Renew ableEnergyWorld.com, November 14, 2005. www.renewableenergyworld.com.
3. Joe Romm, "Hydrogen Fuel Cell Cars Are a Dead End from a Technological, Practical, and Climate Perspective—Chu & Obama Are Right to Kill the Program," Climate Progress, June 11, 2009. http://climateprogress.org.
4. Quoted in Kevin Bullis, "Q & A: Steven Chu," *Technology Review*, May 14, 2009. www.technologyreview.com.
5. Jim Motavalli, "Fuel Cells or Electric Cars?" *Daily Green*, April 28, 2009. www.thedailygreen.com.
6. Electric Power Research Institute, "Environmental Assessment of Plug-In Hybrid Electric Vehicles, Volume 1: Nationwide Greenhouse Gas Emissions," July 2007. http://mydocs.epri.com.
7. Quoted in Mary Knox Merrill, "Worldwide Race to Make Better Batteries," *Christian Science Monitor*, January 22, 2009. www.csmonitor.com.

CHAPTER 7

Achieving a Clean-Energy Economy

Developing the clean-energy technologies that the nation and the world need in order to shift away from fossil fuels will be a huge undertaking—one that involves transforming the carbon-based economy to an economy based on clean energy. Private investments will be crucial to this effort, to provide the investment capital needed to launch clean-energy companies and to sustain these industries over the long term. Many energy experts also believe that this economic shift will require leadership from the government, however, to make policy and economic changes needed to phase out carbon-based fuels and encourage the development and deployment of clean energy and energy efficiency. If successful, numerous economists say this energy transformation will ultimately strengthen the U.S. economy, increase its energy independence, and ensure long-term economic prosperity.

Encouraging Investments in Clean Energy

Financial experts have noted that investments in clean energy tend to be extremely capital intensive—that is, they require large amounts of funding. They also are both high risk and long term, because there has yet to be a robust market for these technologies. As Karl Rábago, chairman of the National Green Power Board, a certifier of green power companies, has explained, "These technologies have paybacks on investment that take 10 or 20 years. . . . So if the market demand is not steady, there will be no capital moving to those facilities."[1] Private investors and venture capitalists, therefore, have historically been reluctant to put money into renewable-energy projects.

Fluctuating oil prices over the years have contributed significantly to the risks of green-power investments by creating a constantly shifting market. When oil prices rise, interest in renewable technologies increases, but when prices drop, the market quickly bottoms out. This scenario occurred in the early 1970s, when the 1973 Arab oil embargo caused oil prices to rise dramatically, inspiring both the private sector and the federal government to invest heavily in new energy technologies in order to decrease U.S. dependence on foreign oil. According to the National Science Foundation, by 1979 combined private and government investment in energy reached more than $10 billion per year. When the oil crisis ended, however, these investments dried up; President Ronald Reagan, for example, slashed government spending for these projects by more than 50 percent.

> *Many energy experts [support] creating a comprehensive new clean-energy policy to reverse U.S. energy policies that have for many years provided support for fossil fuels at the expense of renewable energy.*

Clean-energy investments have been intermittent since then, but the increase in gas prices during the 2007–2008 period, when the price of a barrel of crude oil peaked at $147.30 per gallon, has recently helped to spur a rash of new private clean-energy investments. According to the think tank Center for American Progress, $2.7 billion of venture capital funds in 2007, and $5.9 billion in 2008, were invested in renewable-energy technologies. Global clean-energy investments have also undergone a spike lately. A report prepared for the United Nations Environment Programme's Sustainable Energy Finance Initiative found that close to $155 billion was invested in 2008 in renewable energy companies and projects worldwide—a four-fold increase since 2004. As the report states, "Investment in renewable energy generation projects grew by 13% during 2008, to $117 billion, and new private investment in companies developing and scaling-up

Renewable Energy Portfolio Standards

One way that governments can encourage the growth of renewable energy is by adopting renewable portfolio standards (RPS), also sometimes called renewable electricity standards (RES)—regulations that require utility companies to produce certain percentages of their electricity from renewable energy sources, such as wind, solar, biomass, and geothermal. The goal of these standards is to help create a market for renewables so that costs will come down and green-energy sources will become cost-competitive with fossil fuels. According to the U.S. Environmental Protection Agency (EPA), as of March 2009, thirty-three states plus the District of Columbia have adopted RPS requirements. The state requirements vary in the percentages and types of renewable support required, but most states require between 10 percent and 25 percent of electricity to be produced from renewable sources, and most accept solar, wind, and biomass technologies as qualifying sources of clean energy.

Supporters of this strategy would like to see a strong national RPS. The American Clean Energy and Security Act of 2009—the climate bill passed by the House of Representatives—would create such a federal renewable electricity-standard. Specifically, the legislation requires utility companies that supply more than 4 million megawatts of electricity to produce 20 percent of their electricity from renewable sources by 2020 (and up to 5 percent of this standard could be met through energy efficiency savings). If this or a similar provision is included in a final climate bill and signed by the president, all states would be required to participate.

new technologies increased by 37% from 2007 to $13.5 billion."[2] This growth trend has somewhat reversed; green investments were down in the second half of 2008 and in 2009, due largely to the effects of a worldwide economic recession.

A New Clean-Energy Policy

In order to sustain investors' interest in renewable energy, many energy experts argue that it will be crucial for the U.S. government to send a strong signal that there will be a market for renewables. This can be done in various ways—for example, by creating tax or other incentives for clean-energy companies, by providing subsidies to these industries, or by adopting legislation or regulations that discourage the use of carbon fuels and encourage renewables. In essence, many energy experts say, it means creating a comprehensive new clean-energy policy to reverse U.S. energy policies that have for many years provided support for fossil fuels at the expense of renewable energy. As the Pew Environment Group explains, "Over the past 20 years, federal investments in research and development (R&D) for crude oil and fossil fuels have increased significantly. Meanwhile, R&D in renewable energy has dropped by almost 20% since 1980, and continues to remain stagnant today."[3]

President Barack Obama's administration has set a course in the direction of a clean-energy policy. In addition to pushing for enactment of a climate bill to put a price on carbon, its 2009 economic stimulus package allocated a total of more than $85 billion toward federal and state-level clean-energy programs, loan guarantees, and tax incentives.

The Role of Carbon Caps

Creating a new national energy policy, however, promises to be a difficult political endeavor. Although President Obama succeeded in getting Congress to pass a stimulus bill containing significant government support for renewable energy technologies, he faces strong opposition in his efforts to enact a climate bill and make other more permanent changes to energy policies. This opposition has come from many different quarters—mostly from Republicans and political opponents of the president but also from some environmentalists. Environmental Protection Agency (EPA) lawyers Laurie Williams and Allan Zabel, for example, argue that cap-and-trade legislation will not guarantee reductions in greenhouse gas emissions or spark an energy revolution, as its supporters claim. They state, "The biggest obstacle to this revolution is that uncontrolled fossil fuel energy remains much cheaper than clean energy. Cap-and-trade alone will not create confidence that clean energy will become profitable within a known time frame and so will not ignite the huge shift in investment needed to begin the clean-energy revolution."[4]

Yet proponents of climate legislation insist that a cap-and-trade bill is vitally important to boost private investment in clean energy. Unlike the stimulus bill, which provides direct government spending for clean-energy projects, climate legislation is specifically designed to promote private investment in cleaner energy sources. As clean-energy advocates Richard L. Revesz and Michael A. Livermore argue, "Leveling the playing field by forcing fossil-fuel prices to reflect their true cost will spur a wave of clean-energy investment: research and development in new technologies, new factories to produce solar panels and wind turbines, and energy-efficiency retrofits of commercial and residential real estate."[5] Revesz and Livermore explain that some versions of cap and trade have failed because they gave away permits to high-polluting companies and did not help consumers with rising electricity bills. President Obama's plan, they conclude, avoids these pitfalls.

According to some estimates, the stimulus money and a cap-and-trade law together could generate a massive investment in clean energy and help the United States jump-start the revolution in energy needed for major emission reductions. The Center for American Progress, for example, estimates that these two measures "can generate roughly $150 billion per year in new clean-energy investments in the United States over the next decade. This estimated $150 billion in new spending annually includes government funding but is notably dominated by private-sector investments."[6] With the political support for cap and trade in question, however, other groups such as the think tank Breakthrough Institute have argued that the government should focus on making alternative energy cheaper instead of making fossil fuels expensive. This could be done, they propose, by increasing federal subsidies to approximately $500 billion over the next decade to accelerate clean-energy innovation and development.

Creating Green Jobs

Investments in clean energy, supporters predict, will create a wealth of new "green" jobs in clean-energy companies. In fact, the Center for American Progress claims that clean-energy investments could generate three times more jobs than the same amount of investments in carbon fuels. Specifically, the group estimates that:

> Investments triggered by the economic stimulus program and the forthcoming American Clean Energy and Security Act [a cap-and-trade bill] can generate a net increase of about 1.7 million jobs. . . . These job gains would be enough—on their own—to reduce the unemployment rate in today's economy by about one full percentage point . . . even after taking into full account the inevitable job losses in conventional fossil fuel sectors of the U.S. economy as they contract."[7]

Worldwide, experts predict the numbers could be even greater. A December 2009 report by the Global Climate Network, an alliance of nine progressive think tanks located in various countries, found that clean-energy policies could create as many as 19.7 million high-quality green jobs by 2020. This figure, the group emphasizes, is conservative because it reflects only the jobs potential in eight countries studied. The group noted that strong government support is needed to achieve these job gains.

CLEAN-ENERGY JOBS BY STATE, 2007

| Highest (1.02%–0.82%) | Second smallest (0.62%–0.43%) |
| Second highest (0.81%–0.63%) | Smallest (0.42%–0.24%) |

State	Total Jobs	Percent Clean	State	Total Jobs	Percent Clean	State	Total Jobs	Percent Clean
Alabama	2,193,589	0.36	Kentucky	2,069,602	0.45	North Dakota	422,054	0.50
Alaska	388,361	0.55	Louisiana	2,326,888	0.46	Ohio	6,304,302	0.56
Arizona	2,661,437	0.44	Maine	707,195	0.85	Oklahoma	1,784,492	0.31
Arkansas	1,366,809	0.34	Maryland	3,108,256	0.42	Oregon	1,902,294	1.02
California	17,556,872	0.71	Massachusetts	3,870,356	0.69	Pennsylvania	6,542,137	0.59
Colorado	2,668,069	0.64	Michigan	5,279,234	0.43	Rhode Island	549,754	0.42
Connecticut	2,150,723	0.47	Minnesota	3,143,012	0.64	South Carolina	2,059,151	0.55
Delaware	502,773	0.47	Mississippi	1,356,603	0.24	South Dakota	444,659	0.37
District of Columbia	1,021,958	0.52	Missouri	3,178,657	0.37	Tennessee	3,144,614	0.49
Florida	9,903,922	0.31	Montana	512,093	0.42	Texas	11,726,811	0.47
Georgia	4,955,677	0.33	Nebraska	1,038,673	0.51	Utah	1,291,211	0.40
Hawaii	651,894	0.42	Nevada	1,280,532	0.28	Vermont	365,646	0.59
Idaho	718,373	0.63	New Hampshire	735,051	0.55	Virginia	4,238,337	0.40
Illinois	6,792,326	0.42	New Jersey	4,957,892	0.51	Washington	3,098,042	0.55
Indiana	3,348,351	0.52	New Mexico	970,632	0.50	West Virginia	792,474	0.39
Iowa	1,800,264	0.43	New York	9,964,700	0.34	Wisconsin	3,150,000	0.48
Kansas	1,531,164	0.52	North Carolina	4,629,118	0.37	Wyoming	302,245	0.47

Source: The Pew Charitable Trusts, *The Clean Energy Economy: Repowering Jobs, Businesses and Investments Across America*, Washington, DC: The Pew Charitable Trusts, 2009.

Not everyone agrees that green jobs will lift the economy, however. Many opponents of the clean-energy agenda point to a March 2009 study by Gabriel Calzada of the Universidad Rey Juan Carlos in Madrid, Spain, which found that government subsidies for renewable energy create an artificial market that loses more jobs than it creates. Specifically Calzada's study found that Spain's $8 billion annual investments in clean energy have led to 2.2 job losses economy-wide for every green job created. Each of these green jobs, Calzada concluded, cost Spain $774,000. The result for Spain, Calzada supporters say, has been a rising unemployment rate and a sluggish economy. Critics such as the *Wall Street Journal*, however, have blamed Calzada for failing to identify which jobs were lost and for being less than objective about green initiatives, because Calzada is the founder of a libertarian think tank funded by ExxonMobil, an oil company.

Economic Impact

The Calzada study focused attention on what may be the core challenge facing all who hope to create a clean-energy economy—how to make the transition to clean energy without hurting the U.S. and global economies. Economists disagree strongly about the economic impact of a cap-and-trade bill, with some arguing that it would be a negative economic shock and others viewing it as an essential tool to stimulate the sagging economy. Economics professor Sergey V. Mityakov cautions that cap and trade could damage the U.S. economy, stating:

> If cap and trade were created now, it would lead to higher energy prices for American consumers and businesses, as energy producers would be forced to switch from cheaper and "dirty" fuels such as coal to "cleaner" and more expensive sources of energy. . . . On the one hand, consumers are going to suffer

---

Following page: Workers install solar electric panels in California, an example of green jobs. David McNew/Getty Images.

directly from the increased prices of the energy and energy-intensive goods they buy. On the other hand, higher energy prices will increase the production costs of American producers, making American-produced goods less competitive in the world market. This would tend to make the current recession even more severe, as [many] businesses, which cannot compete against foreign producers, would close. Facing increased energy costs and competition from abroad, some American companies would have an incentive to shift their production overseas where no cap-and-trade system is operating. These adverse effects on producers are likely to lead to additional job losses in the United States, further increasing the costs of the recession for the American households.[8]

Similarly, Ben Lieberman, an economic analyst for the Heritage Foundation, a conservative think tank, has argued that the cap-and-trade bill enacted by the House "reduces gross domestic product by an average of $393 billion annually between 2012 and 2035, and cumulatively by $9.4 trillion."[9]

On the other side of this debate, Mark Tercek, president of the Nature Conservancy, argues that cap and trade will provide a necessary foundation for future economic growth:

Contrary to what may be a developing strain of conventional wisdom, strong policies to reduce climate emissions, such as a market-based cap on U.S. greenhouse emissions, can provide a form of stimulus to the U.S. economy. As during the Great Depression and other recessions, the U.S. economy is suffering from a shortfall in aggregate demand—the collective willingness of American consumers and businesses to buy goods and services. . . . Today, by driving private investment in zero- and low-carbon technologies and boots-on-the-ground conservation efforts to reduce net carbon emissions, a national market-based cap on carbon that tightens over time can act as a long-term driver for demand. A cap-and-trade system will not only lower emissions and fight climate change, but also will stimulate the economy.[10]

Still other economists admit that a cap-and-trade bill would have some economic costs but claim it would be worth it in the long run. Economist Paul Krugman declares, for example, "Yes, limiting emissions would have its costs. As a card-carrying economist, I cringe when 'green economy' enthusiasts insist that protecting the environment would be all gain, no pain. But the best available estimates suggest that the costs of an emissions-limitation program would be modest, as long as it's implemented gradually. And committing ourselves now might actually help the economy recover from its current slump."[11]

Fear about economic costs, however, is only one of the challenges to be faced as the United States and other countries begin to make the transition to cleaner energy sources. Numerous other potential obstacles lie ahead.

Notes

1. Quoted in Damien Cave, "Green Power in the Red," *Salon*, January 18, 2001. www.salon.com.
2. United Nations Environment Programme, "Global Trends in Sustainable Energy Investment," Executive Summary, 2009. http://sefi.unep.org.
3. Pew Environment Group, "Developing the Clean-Energy Economy That America Needs Will Require Greater Investments in Renewable Energy Technologies," 2009. www.pewtrusts.org.
4. Laurie Williams and Allan Zabel, "Cap-and-Trade Mirage," *Washington Post*, October 31, 2009. www.washingtonpost.com.
5. Richard L. Revesz and Michael A. Livermore, "Obama's Carbon Cap-and-Trade Plan Can Boost Growth," *BusinessWeek*, March 10, 2009. www.businessweek.com.
6. Robert Pollin, James Heintz, Heidi Garrett-Peltier, "The Economic Benefits of Investing in Clean Energy," Center for American Progress, June 18, 2009. www.americanprogress.org.
7. Pollin et al., "The Economic Benefits of Investing in Clean Energy."
8. Quoted in Toni Johnson, "Cap and Trade's Economic Impact," Council on Foreign Relations, March 19, 2009. www.cfr.org/publication.
9. Ben Lieberman, "The Economic Impact of the Waxman-Markey Cap-and-Trade Bill," Testimony Before the Senate Republican Conference, June 22, 2009. www.heritage.org.
10. Quoted in Johnson, "Cap and Trade's Economic Impact."
11. Paul Krugman, "An Affordable Salvation," *New York Times*, April 30, 2009. www.nytimes.com.

Chapter 8

Challenges in the Search for Clean Energy

The debate about the economic impact of clean-energy initiatives illustrates the great difficulty of making fundamental changes to energy policy. Moving to a carbon-free society and creating an energy revolution will involve many other problems as well—everything from solving technological issues inherent in making new energy technologies practicable and cost-competitive, to rebuilding outmoded energy infrastructure, and addressing serious political, social, and international concerns. Confronting these challenges will be the work of today's leaders, and the countries that succeed in finding the right solutions, many commentators say, will become the global superpowers of tomorrow.

Technological Challenges

Because most clean-energy technologies, such as solar, wind, geothermal, and biomass, are still in the development phase, scientists and researchers still need to find the answers to a variety of technical questions critical to moving these technologies into mass production and large-scale implementation. U.S. energy secretary Steven Chu predicts that it will take major breakthroughs in at least three core clean-energy technologies—electric batteries for vehicles, new perennial crops to create biofuels, and affordable solar panels that will not require government subsidies—to reach the goal of converting the United States to alternative energy. As Secretary Chu has stated, "We effectively need a second industrial revolution that gives us the energy we need, allows us to use it as efficiently as possible [and does not pollute the climate]."[1]

The effort to develop more powerful batteries to run electric cars provides a good example of these technological challenges. Despite many recent advances in battery technology, car manufacturers still need a better battery to truly revolutionize the industry. The lithium-ion battery appears to be the leading candidate, and it is the battery technology used in new hybrids such as the General Motors Volt. Improvements may be on the horizon, however. In 2007 Stanford University scientist Yi Cui found a way to increase the storage capacity of current lithium-ion batteries tenfold by using silicon nanowires. Energy experts say it will take years, however, before this advancement can be applied to electric cars and made available for purchase.

Similar technological challenges must be confronted to perfect other clean-energy technologies. Technologies such as solar, biomass, wind, geothermal, hydrogen, and water are all clearing hurdles to become a prominent part of the future energy landscape, and each will require further development before it can be considered a practical alternative to fossil fuels.

Infrastructure Needs

Once these green technologies become viable, the United States may need to upgrade its electrical transmission infrastructure in order to transmit clean electricity to consumers. Most experts agree that the current U.S. electrical grid, which dates to the 1960s, is fragmented, out of date, inefficient, and incapable of properly transmitting electricity from renewable energy plants to homes around the country. The grid even has trouble handling today's increasing electricity demands, as evidenced by a number of widespread power disruptions, or blackouts, in recent years.

What is needed, many energy experts say, is a new smart electricity grid—digitized, so that it can be controlled by computers;

TODAY'S ELECTRICAL GRID AND TOMORROW'S

Characteristic	Today's Grid	Smart Grid
Enables active participation by consumers	Consumers are uninformed and non-participative with power system	Informed, involved, and active consumers—demand response and distributed energy resources
Accommodates all generation and storage options	Dominated by central generation—many obstacles exist for distributed energy resources interconnection	Many distributed energy resources with plug-and-play convenience—focus on renewables
Enables new products, services, and markets	Limited wholesale markets, not well integrated—limited opportunities for consumers	Mature, well-integrated wholesale markets, growth of new electricity markets for consumers
Provides power quality for the digital economy	Focus on outages—slow response to power quality issues	Power quality is a priority with a variety of quality/price options—rapid resolution of issues
Optimizes assets and operates efficiently	Little integration of operational data with asset management—business process silos	Greatly expanded data acquisition of grid parameters—focus on prevention, minimizing impact to consumers
Anticipates and responds to system disturbances (self-heals)	Responds to prevent further damage—focus is on protecting assets following fault	Automatically detects and responds to problems—focus on prevention, minimizing impact to consumers
Operates resiliently against attack and natural disaster	Vulnerable to malicious acts of terror and natural disasters	Resilient to attack and natural disasters with rapid restoration capabilities

Source: U.S. Department of Energy, *The Smart Grid: An Introduction*, October 2008. www.oe.energy.gov.

capable of handling intermittent types of energy, such as wind and solar; and connected on a nationwide basis to maximize energy efficiency. A smart grid system would also provide for two-way communication between homes and power sources, so that usage could be adjusted to prevent blackouts and direct electricity wherever it is needed most. Such a smart electricity grid, experts say, is vital to implementing a green-energy revolution. As Jesse Berst, director of the energy research group GlobalSmartEnergy, explains, "The ultimate result stemming from a new digitized electricity grid will be a move away from petroleum-based fuels. Once the new electric infrastructure is up and running, we will be able to deploy a host of fuel sources—renewable and non-renewable—for the first time on a large-scale basis."[2]

In the 2009 economic stimulus bill, Congress allocated $4.5 billion for smart grid technology, but this amount will provide only a start. A recent report by the think tank Electric Power Research Institute projects that the total cost of building a nationwide smart grid could reach $165 billion, or about $8 billion a year for two decades. And cost is not the only obstacle. Some commentators say the bigger problem is getting all affected parties—the electric power industry, electric car manufacturers, and individual states—to agree on standards and details of implementation. A January 2010 U.S. Supreme Court decision not to review a lower court ruling that upheld states' rights to deny permits for new transmission lines only adds to these difficulties. The lower court held that the Federal Energy Regulatory Commission (FERC) does not have the authority under current law to approve a transmission project that a state regulatory commission has previously denied. Critics say this decision will allow states, if they so choose, to prevent both the federal government and private companies from building new smart grid transmission lines. Yet another issue is security; computer experts warn that a nationwide computerized electrical grid could easily be targeted by hackers, unless stringent security standards are required.

Political Obstacles

The technological barriers, however, pale when compared to the political obstacles facing leaders and experts who are trying to push for a clean-energy agenda. Members of Congress, whether Democrats or Republicans, representing states or districts that are home to fossil fuel industries or companies that use large amounts of fossil fuels feel pressure to oppose any measures, such as cap and trade or carbon taxes, that might make dirty energy more expensive. The fact that the nation is still mired in a deep recession hardens this opposition because constituents are worried about job losses and rising energy prices.

Recent polls confirm that the public's fears about the economy may override their fears about global warming. A January 2010 poll by the Pew Research Center for the People and the Press, for example, found that Americans rated strengthening the economy and improving the job situation their highest priorities (83 percent and 81 percent, respectively), while rating protecting the environment and dealing with global warming as low priorities (44 percent and 28 percent, respectively). As the Pew Center explains, "Dealing with global warming ranks at the bottom of the public's list of priorities; just 28% consider this a top priority, the lowest measure for any issue tested in the survey. . . . [This percentage] has fallen 10 points from 2007, when 38% considered it a top priority."[3]

Yet at the same time, public support for clean-energy policies may be at an all-time high. In a March 2009 poll by the Center for American Progress, 76 percent of respondents agreed that "America's economic future requires a transformation away from oil, gas, and coal to renewable energy sources such as wind and solar."[4] Progressives hope that this growing support for clean energy will allow the federal government to move forward with stimulus investments in green energy, and perhaps more permanent subsidies and regulatory actions, regardless of whether carbon cuts are politically possible.

As many commentators have noted, President Barack Obama's strategy is to frame green initiatives as jobs programs and efforts to stimulate the economy. The 2009 economic stimulus bill, for example, was presented as a nationwide effort to create a million new jobs, jump-start economic growth, and transform the U.S. economy for the twenty-first century. Obama's proposed fiscal year 2011 budget continues this effort. According to analysts, for 2011, the president proposes to add $833 million in green spending above levels in the 2010 budget—monies that would be additional to those included in the stimulus spending. The proposed budget also eliminates $36.5 billion in taxpayer subsidies (for the period 2011 to 2020) for big oil companies such as BP, Chevron, ConocoPhillips, ExxonMobil, and Shell—companies that reportedly earned $67 billion in profits during 2009.

Whether President Obama can succeed in his effort to remake the U.S. economy into one powered by clean energy remains to be seen. Many environmentalists are pleased with his progress so far. As Center for American Pogress climate strategy director Daniel Weiss notes, the president's clean-energy accomplishments in 2009 are "a startling achievement amidst the worst economy in 70 years, two wars, and an opposition party disinterested in cooperation."[5]

Environmental Concerns

As clean-energy projects are built, many observers expect another type of opposition to emerge—environmental objections. Already, some clean-energy projects have encountered complaints about location and their effects on surrounding residents, area wildlife, and the environment. As reporter Stephanie Tavares explains:

> Hydropower and the dams that come with [it] interrupt the natural flow of rivers and the migration and breeding of native fish; geothermal plants require water and their exploratory drilling sometimes damages the land; modern wind farms kill migratory birds and bats and kick up dust during construction; utility-scale solar photovoltaic [PV] arrays are made

from sometimes toxic or unsustainably mined materials and require vast expanses of land formerly open to native animals; and solar thermal plants face the same land use issues as solar PV but also can't operate without a good deal of water.[6]

Environmentalists and residents also have objected to plans to build new transmission lines to connect renewable energy projects, which are often in rural areas, to populations in big cities. The main objection is that the routes for these lines often cross migration lanes needed by endangered species for grazing and mating, but local residents also sometimes object to electrical lines spoiling their scenic vistas. As environmental lawyer Rick Campbell explains, "Everybody is so behind green energy until the wind turbine goes up on the ridge behind your house. . . . Even though in the long run it's a clean type of energy compared to coal, you still have (significant) environmental issues related to these types of energy. . . . There is no kind of project that has no impact on anyone."[7]

Although the United States has been slow to move toward renewables, it is clear that many other countries have already decided to make big investments in clean energy.

A classic example of this type of conflict between utilities and environmentalists is Sempra Energy's Sunrise Powerlink transmission project—a proposal to build 150 miles (241.4 km) of new high-voltage electrical lines from southern California's desert to San Diego in order to connect solar and geothermal plants with end users. The transmission line would traverse 20 miles of a national forest and affect other public and private lands that environmentalists believe should be protected as pristine, scenic backcountry regions. Although the California Public Utilities Commission has approved the project, observers say legal challenges from opponents could still delay construction or stop it completely.

The Sunrise Powerlink project raises yet another critical green-energy issue that is simmering within the environmental movement—should solar energy be generated by large, concentrated power plants built and run by utility companies or should energy production be decentralized and produced by multiple local facilities and homeowners? Many energy experts argue that decentralized energy production is not feasible considering the growing demand for electricity. Supporters disagree, claiming local production would be cheaper and could produce enough electricity to avoid the environmental concerns associated with new transmission lines. As David Morris, vice president of the Institute for Local Self-Reliance, argues: "Before we build high voltage transmission lines we should harness all available distributed renewable resources and maximize the efficiency of existing transmission and distribution lines. How much electricity could we generate in this fashion? The jury is still out, but increasing evidence suggests it could be very significant."[8]

Winning the Global Race Toward Clean Energy

Because climate change is truly a global problem, the United States also faces the dual challenge of both coordinating and competing with various foreign nations during the shift away from fossil fuels. On the one hand, international cooperation is essential because every nation must reduce greenhouse gas (GHG) emissions in order for global carbon levels to decrease. On the other hand, the United States is facing serious economic challenges from China and other countries in the race to develop renewable energy technologies. Although the United States has been slow to move toward renewables, it is clear that many other countries have already decided to make big investments in clean energy. In fact, a November 2009 report released by two think tanks, the Breakthrough Institute and the Information Technology and Innovation Foundation, finds that three Asian nations—China, Japan, and South Korea—have already passed the United

China and Clean Energy

Even though China's enormous energy needs are expected to keep it dependent on coal for up to 70 percent of its energy needs over the next couple of decades, China is also fast becoming a leading investor in clean, renewable energy technologies. Recent reports indicate that China spent $16.7 billion on clean energy in 2008—for the first time surpassing the United States in this area. Many experts say that China is now positioned to become the world leader in green technologies such as solar, wind, and biomass. The Chinese government has plans to invest $217 billion over the next five years, an amount that dwarfs the approximately $85 billion dedicated to promoting clean energy in the U.S. economic stimulus legislation. And experts are fairly confident that China can reach its goal of deriving at least 15 percent of its energy from renewable sources by 2020. China is already the leading manufacturer of solar photovoltaic panels, but it recently adopted an aggressive solar power plan aimed at boosting solar even more. Extra spending and support is also being provided to other renewable technologies, including nuclear and wind power. By 2020, for example, the Chinese government hopes to increase the country's wind power eight times current levels. Investment in a new electricity transmission grid is also part of the Chinese plan. Experts say that China's massive investments in green energy pose a great economic challenge to the United States, because China and not the United States could become the leading manufacturer of green tech products—a major global industry of the future.

States in producing almost all the clean-energy technologies. Direct government investments by these countries in clean-energy research, manufacturing, and deployment, the report concludes, will give them market advantage over U.S. companies and could jeopardize long-term U.S. economic competitiveness. The report warns that if the United States hopes to compete in this area it must act quickly to provide much more support for U.S. clean-technology research.

President Obama agrees with this assessment. In a 2009 speech to Congress, he declared:

> We know the country that harnesses the power of clean, renewable energy will lead the 21st century. And yet, it is China that has launched the largest effort in history to make their economy energy efficient. We invented solar technology, but we've fallen behind countries like Germany and Japan in producing it. New plug-in hybrids roll off our assembly lines, but they will run on batteries made in Korea. Well I do not accept a future where the jobs and industries of tomorrow take root beyond our borders—and I know you don't either. It is time for America to lead again.[9]

President Obama has pressed this issue many times since then, including in his January 27, 2010, State of the Union address, in which he reiterated, "The nation that leads the clean-energy economy will be the nation that leads the global economy, and America must be that nation."[10]

In the end, therefore, one often forgotten challenge raised by global warming may be the competition from other nations in clean energy—a threat that could jeopardize the nation's future economic prosperity as well as its standing in the world.

Notes

1. Quoted in Jesse Jenkins, "Energy Secretary Steven Chu: Honorary Breakthrough Fellow?" *Breakthrough Blog*, February 12, 2009. www.thebreakthrough.org.
2. Jesse Berst, "Electronomics: Why We Need Smart Grid Technology and Infrastructure Today," *Xconomy*, February 12, 2009. www.xconomy.com.
3. Pew Center for People and the Press, "Public's Priorities for 2010: Economy, Jobs, Terrorism," January 25, 2010. http://people-press.org.
4. Quoted in Ruy Teixeira, "Public Opinion Snapshot: Strong Support for Clean-Energy Economy," Center for American Progress, March 30, 2009. www.american progress .org.
5. Daniel J. Weiss, "A Breath of Fresh Air: Obama Seizes the Energy Opportunity," Center for American Progress, February 11, 2010. www.americanprogress.org.

6. Stephanie Tavares, "Environmental Concerns Roadblock to Renewable Energy," *Las Vegas Sun*, February 6, 2009. www.lasvegassun.com.

7. Quoted in Tavares, "Environmental Concerns Roadblock to Renewable Energy."

8. David Morris, "Distributed Energy First, Wait on New Transmission Lines," renewableenergyworld.com, April 28, 2008. www.renewableenergyworld.com.

9. Barack Obama, "Remarks of President Barack Obama—As Prepared for Delivery Address to Joint Session of Congress," February 24, 2009. www.whitehouse.gov.

10. Barack Obama, "Remarks by the President in State of the Union Address," The White House, Office of the Press Secretary, January 27, 2010. www.whitehouse.gov.

CHAPTER 9

Conclusion

The threat of global climate change is clearly pushing the world toward a critical juncture in human history—a turning point in energy that could affect the fate of nations and even human civilization. As the International Energy Agency, an intergovernmental organization that advises twenty-eight member countries on energy issues, states in its World Energy Outlook 2008, "It is not an exaggeration to claim that the future of human prosperity depends on how successfully we tackle the two central energy challenges facing us today: securing the supply of reliable and affordable energy; and effecting a rapid transformation to a low-carbon, efficient and environmentally benign system of energy supply."[1]

There is widespread agreement that this energy revolution requires a dedicated effort at all governmental levels. Yet, more than at any other time in recent history, the political will to address climate change and spur clean-energy innovation seems to be declining. Skepticism about global warming appears to be higher than ever in some quarters, and the collapse of the Copenhagen talks, many people think, may signal the end of United Nations–sponsored, Kyoto-type international agreements mandating global emissions reductions. Without this mandate, there is a danger that many countries, especially ones in the developing world such as China, may fail to make meaningful cuts in greenhouse gas emissions. And in the United States, President

Barack Obama's own hopes of achieving emissions cuts with carbon cap legislation seem to have weakened significantly since he took office.

On the other hand, research is under way on a vast array of low- and zero-emission technologies, and the pace of innovation is so fast that almost every day seems to bring new reports of ideas and possible breakthroughs. In fact, aided recently by increased funding from private investors and many governments, scientists and engineers around the world are pushing ahead on a wealth of ideas that promise to improve solar, wind, geothermal, biofuel, hydrogen, electric battery, and other renewable types of energy. Many of these technologies may be only a few years away from the point where they can be mass-produced and put to use as part of the global energy system. Visionary thinkers and researchers, too, have already proposed multiple ways to implement these technologies to reach the main goal—reducing emissions to the level needed to avoid catastrophic climate change.

If the United States chooses to strongly embrace this trend toward clean energy, many experts say the results could be dramatic. As the Basic Energy Sciences Advisory Committee states in a December 2008 report to the U.S. Department of Energy:

> Recall a time of similar peril on the verge of World War II when President Franklin D. Roosevelt launched a wave of national investment into what were at the time unproven approaches, leading to the massive mobilization of scientists, engineers, and industrialists that led to radar, harnessing the power of the atom and other technologies—and the scientific base on which they rested—that gave the U.S. a decisive edge, not just in war, but in the global peacetime economy that followed. Might a similar science and technology mobilization be just what is needed to address today's problems? Could it help jump-start the economy and generate millions of new jobs in an expanding sustainable energy industry? Free the U.S. from the national security threats and the huge drain on our economy of imported oil? Reclaim our national reputa-

tion and our global technology leadership with a revolutionary wave of clean energy technologies that address the threat of global climate change and capture the burgeoning global market for high technology energy solutions? Just as with the Manhattan Project or the later Apollo effort to reach the moon, the outcome is not certain, but the prospects—grounded in remarkable new capabilities for controlling complex materials and chemical processes, growing entrepreneurial enthusiasm, and careful scientific assessments of what might be achieved—are . . . breathtaking.[2]

At this point, however, the direction of the United States is still in flux, and no one is certain about which technologies will develop the fastest, how they might work together, or what might emerge as the best strategy for each country. The global energy future still seems uncertain, even as climate experts warn that the world is fast running out of time and that only a narrow window exists for effective action on global warming. What is certain is that the population of the earth is facing a major shift in energy usage that is bound to bring upheaval as well as progress. Once this process begins in earnest, many commentators predict, rapid change will be seen comparable in scale to that brought by the Industrial Revolution—change that will fundamentally alter and improve the lives of most people on the globe. In the face of such great change, which causes many people to fear for themselves and their children, it is important to remember the end goal—a sustainable energy future where dirty and unsustainable fossil fuels are a distant memory, renewable resources meet most of the world's energy needs, and energy usage no longer pollutes the environment or threatens human existence.

Notes

1. International Energy Agency, "World Energy Outlook 2008," Executive Summary. www.worldenergyoutlook.org.
2. Basic Energy Sciences Advisory Committee, "New Science for a Secure and Sustainable Energy Future," December 2008. www.er.doe.gov.

Glossary

atmosphere The gaseous envelope surrounding the earth.

biodiesel A type of diesel fuel produced from soybeans and other biomass that produces fewer emissions than petroleum diesel.

biofuel A fuel produced from biomass, such as municipal solid waste, agricultural crops, and trees and plants. Examples of biofuel include ethanol and biodiesel.

biomass Organic matter, either living or dead, such as trees and plants, as well as municipal solid waste.

CAFE standards The Corporate Average Fuel Economy (CAFE) regulations in the United States, first enacted by the U.S. Congress in 1975, that are intended to improve the average fuel economy of cars and light trucks (trucks, vans, and sport-utility vehicles) sold in the United States.

cap and trade A system that sets an overall limit on the amount of allowable greenhouse gas emissions and allows countries or companies that cannot meet emissions reduction targets to buy carbon credits from other countries or companies that are exceeding emissions reduction goals.

carbon cap A limit on the amount of carbon dioxide that a country or company is permitted to release into the atmosphere.

carbon dioxide (CO_2) A gas formed during respiration, combustion, and organic decomposition; one of the greenhouse gases that contribute to global warming.

carbon sequestration The process of capturing carbon dioxide before it enters the atmosphere and permanently storing it in deep underground formations or under ocean waters.

carbon tax An environmental tax on emissions of carbon dioxide.

Clean Air Act The federal law that regulates air emissions in the United States and gives authority to the Environmental Protection Agency (EPA) for protecting and improving the nation's air quality and the stratospheric ozone layer.

clean coal Technologies used to burn coal more efficiently and release significantly fewer gaseous emissions into the atmosphere. One of these technologies is carbon sequestration.

clean energy A term used to describe sources of energy that are environmentally friendly and that produce no or few greenhouse gas emissions.

climate change Long-term global weather changes caused by global warming.

crude oil Liquid petroleum found in underground deposits formed by the decomposition of plants and animals that lived hundreds of millions of years ago; one of the fossil fuels.

deforestation The removal of forested land and its conversion into roads, agricultural land, or some other kind of non-forested land.

electric car A type of automobile that runs on electricity. Some electric cars run only on electricity, whereas others (hybrid electric vehicles) have both a gasoline and an electric motor.

emissions The release of greenhouse gases into the atmosphere from the burning of fossil fuels and various other sources that cause global warming.

emissions trading (also called carbon trading) A market mechanism that allows emitters (countries, companies, or facilities) to buy emissions credits from or sell emissions credits to other emitters.

energy efficiency A measure of how much energy is used versus how much energy is wasted.

Energy Star A program started by the United States government in 1992 in which certain appliances are rated and given an "Energy Star" label for being very energy efficient.

ethanol An alternative automobile fuel produced using corn or other biomass.

feedback loop A process in which one condition creates other conditions that reinforce the first.

fossil fuel A hydrocarbon deposit, such as petroleum, coal, or natural gas, created in underground deposits hundreds of millions of years ago from the decomposition of plants and animals.

fuel economy The relationship between distance traveled by an automobile and the amount of fuel it consumed.

geoengineering Human manipulation of global climate mechanisms that is intended to slow global warming.

geothermal energy Heat energy that is continuously produced below the earth's crust from a layer of hot and molten rock called magma.

glacier A year-round mass of ice that is located on, and moves across, land.

global warming An increase in the average temperature of the earth's atmosphere and ocean that can cause climate changes.

green jobs Jobs created in industries engaged in researching, producing, selling, or installing clean-energy technologies.

greenhouse effect The process in which certain gases in the atmosphere, that is, greenhouse gases, trap energy from the sun and warm the earth.

greenhouse gases (GHG) Those gaseous constituents of the atmosphere, both natural and anthropogenic, that trap energy from the sun and warm the earth. The Kyoto Protocol refers specifically to the following six GHGs: carbon dioxide, methane, nitrous oxide, hydrofluorocarbons, perfluorocarbons, and sulfur hexafluoride.

hydrogen fuel cell A device that produces electricity through a chemical reaction—by combining hydrogen with oxygen—and yields water as a by-product.

hydropower (also called hydroelectric power) Power produced by capturing the energy in moving streams and rivers.

Industrial Revolution The massive economic and social change begun in the 1700s brought about when machines replaced manual labor and animal power, and fossil fuels replaced wind, water, and wood as sources of energy.

Intergovernmental Panel on Climate Change (IPCC) Established in 1988 by the World Meteorological Organization and the UN Environment Programme, the IPCC is a scientific body charged with providing the world a clear scientific view on the current state of climate change and its potential environmental and socioeconomic consequences.

Kyoto Protocol An international agreement adopted in December 1997 in Kyoto, Japan. The protocol sets binding emission targets for developed countries that would reduce their emissions on average to 5.2 percent below 1990 levels.

lithium-ion battery Disposable, rechargeable battery that uses lithium metal or compounds and can store twice the amount of energy stored by today's standard nickel-metal-hydride batteries.

methane A flammable gas produced by decomposition of organic matter; one of the greenhouse gases that causes global warming.

methane hydrates A type of flammable ice that forms when methane gas from the decomposition of organic material comes into contact with water at low temperatures and high pressures.

mitigation Techniques or processes that reduce or offset the adverse impacts of climate change.

nanoengineered Materials engineered at microscopic levels.

NASA National Aeronautics and Space Administration, a U.S. government agency responsible for aviation and spaceflight.

natural gas A gaseous, flammable form of petroleum largely made up of methane; a fossil fuel.

nitrous oxide (NO) A gas emitted as a by-product of combustion; one of the greenhouse gases that causes global warming.

nuclear power Energy derived from nuclear fission, a process that involves splitting atoms of uranium rather than the burning of fossil fuels.

photovoltaic (PV) solar A type of solar energy production that employs semiconductor devices, often made of silicon, that convert light directly into electricity.

reforestation Planting of forests on lands that have previously supported forests but that were converted to some other type of land.

renewable energy Power derived from a natural source that is renewable over a human lifetime; examples include solar power, wind power, biomass power, and hydroelectric power.

renewable portfolio standard A government program that requires utilities to generate a certain amount of energy from renewable energy sources.

smart electricity grid An advanced, computer-run system for transmitting and distributing electricity to consumers that uses two-way digital technology in order to increase efficiency.

solar energy Power derived from the sun's rays.

sustainable Capable of being used without long-term damage to the environment.

tidal energy Power produced from the rise and fall of ocean tides.

wave energy Power produced from surface ocean waves.

wind power Energy produced from wind.

For Further Research

Books

Ron Bowman, *The Green Guide to Power: Thinking Outside the Grid*. Charleston, SC: BookSurge, 2008.
>   Discusses the global energy crisis and the need for new alternative energy sources.

Travis Bradford and John Rubino, *Solar Revolution: The Economic Transformation of the Global Energy Industry*. Cambridge, MA: MIT Press, 2008.
>   Lays out a positive vision of how the solar industry will revolutionize the global energy economy.

Robert Galvin and Kurt Yeager, *Perfect Power: How the Microgrid Revolution Will Unleash Cleaner, Greener, More Abundant Energy*. New York: McGraw-Hill, 2008.
>   Argues that there is an urgent need to upgrade and modernize the U.S. electric grid through integrated microgrids.

Clark W. Gellings, *The Smart Grid: Enabling Energy Efficiency and Demand Response*. Boca Raton, FL: CRC Press, 2009.
>   Explains how various new technologies can be used to create a new "smart grid" electrical system in the United States.

Robert Hefner, *The Grand Energy Transition: The Rise of Energy Gases, Sustainable Life and Growth, and the Next Great Economic Expansion*. New York: Wiley, 2009.
>   Presents an energy plan that would encourage the use of natural gas, solar, wind, and hydrogen.

Miriam Horn and Fred Krupp, *Earth: The Sequel: The Race to Reinvent Energy and Stop Global Warming*. New York: W.W. Norton, 2009.
>   Argues for strict carbon caps as a market-based way to address climate change.

Jeane Manning and Joel Garbon, *Breakthrough Power: How Quantum-Leap New Energy Inventions Can Transform Our World*. Vancouver, Canada: Amber Bridge, 2009.
Reviews innovative new clean-technology developments that could change the world of energy.

Richard Munson, *From Edison to Enron: The Business of Power and What It Means for the Future of Electricity*. New York: Praeger, 2008.
Provides a history of the electric power industry.

Brian O'Leary, *The Energy Solution Revolution*. Lancaster, UK: Bridger House, 2008.
Discusses the current status and future promise of clean energy research.

Ron Pernick and Clint Wilder, *The Clean Tech Revolution: Discover the Top Trends, Technologies, and Companies to Watch*. New York: Harper, 2008.
Discusses the eight major clean-tech sectors and how people can profit from them.

John Rubino, *Clean Money: Picking Winners in the Green Tech Boom*. New York: Wiley, 2008.
Provides an introduction to the world of clean technology and the wealth boom it is likely to create.

Benjamin K. Sovacool, *The Dirty Energy Dilemma: What's Blocking Clean Power in the United States*. Westport, CT: Praeger, 2008.
Examines why wind, solar, and other clean-power technologies have not been developed more quickly to produce electricity in the United States.

Gabrielle Walker and Sir David King, *The Hot Topic*. New York: Harcourt, 2008.
Provides a concise guide to global warming and proposed solutions.

Charles Weiss and William B. Bonvillian, *Structuring an Energy Technology Revolution*. Cambridge, MA: MIT Press, 2009.

Offers a four-step plan for how America's policy makers can encourage innovation and development of sustainable and affordable clean energy.

Periodicals

David Biello, "IEA: Energy Revolution Required to Combat Climate Change," *Scientific American*, December 17, 2009. www.scientificamerican.com.

Karlyn Bowman, "Public Cooling on Global Warming," *Forbes*, December 21, 2009. www.forbes.com.

Rana Foroohar, "The Coming Energy Wars," *Newsweek*, June 9, 2008. www.newsweek.com.

Michael Grunwald, "America's Untapped Energy Resource: Boosting Efficiency," *Time*, December 31, 2008. www.time .com.

Steven F. Hayward, "The EPA's Power Grab," *Weekly Standard*, December 28, 2009. www.weeklystandard.com.

Peter Jackson, "From Stockholm to Kyoto: A Brief History of Climate Change," *UN Chronicle*, vol. 44, no. 2, June 2007, p. 6.

Rachael King, "The Coming Energy Revolution," *BusinessWeek*, October 15, 2009. www.msnbc.msn.com.

William Pentland, "Green Giants: The World's Biggest Clean-Energy Projects," *Forbes*, April 30, 2008. www.forbes.com.

Max Schulz, "The Quiet Energy Revolution," *The American*, February 4, 2010. www.american.com.

Stefan Schultz, "Germany's Coming Energy Revolution," *BusinessWeek*, October 16, 2009. www.businessweek.com.

Robert Socolow and Stephen Pacala, "A Plan to Keep Carbon in Check," *Scientific American*, no. 295, September 2006, pp. 50–57.

Devon Swezey, "Beyond 'Buy American': The U.S. Needs a Clean Energy Strategy," *Forbes*, March 8, 2010. http://blogs .forbes.com.

William Underhill, "The Next Industrial Revolution," *Newsweek*, December 14, 2009. www.newsweek.com.

Vivienne Walt, "After the Recession, an Energy Crisis Could Loom," *Time*, November 10, 2009. www.time.com.

Zareed Zakaria, "Free at Last: How to Achieve Genuine Energy Independence," *Newsweek*, April 13, 2009. www.newsweek .com.

Internet Sources

Christopher Beam, "Hot in Here: You Thought the Health Care Battle Was Ugly. Just Wait for the Climate Fight," *Slate*, August 28, 2009. www.slate.com.

Nick Chambers, "Brazil's 10 Millionth Ethanol Flex-Fuel Vehicle Hits the Road," Reuters, March 9, 2010. www.reuters .com.

Mark Clayton, "Energy Efficiency Can Deliver Big Rewards," *Christian Science Monitor*, May 1, 2009. www.csmonitor .com.

Mark Clayton, "Governors Prod Washington on Renewable Energy," *Christian Science Monitor*, March 16, 2010. www .csmonitor.com.

Herman Daly, "From a Failed-Growth Economy to a Steady-State Economy," *Solutions*, February 10, 2010. www.the solutionsjournal.com.

Jim Efstathiou Jr., "Copenhagen Failure Defied by $200 Billion in Green Investments," *Bloomberg.com*, December 2, 2009. www.bloomberg.com.

Josh Freed, Avi Zevin, and Jesse Jenkins, "Jump-starting a Clean Energy Revolution," *Breakthrough Institute*, September 2009. http://thebreakthrough.org.

Jennifer M. Granholm, "A Clean Energy Triple Play," *Huffington Post*, February 25, 2010. www.huffingtonpost.com.

Daniel Gross, "Denver's Secret: Why So Many Green Jobs Are Sprouting in Colorado," *Slate*, June 27, 2009. www.slate .com/id.

Daniel Gross, "The Real 'Green' Innovation: Why Alternative Energy Depends More on Financial Wizardry than Mechanical Wizardry," *Slate*, April 16, 2009. www.slate.com.

H. Josef Hebert, "How the Climate Bill May Spur an Energy Revolution," *Huffington Post*, June 27, 2009. www .huffingtonpost.com.

Richard Heinberg, "Is 'Clean Coal' a Dead End," *Post Carbon Institute*, December 10, 2009. www.postcarbon.org.

Christina Larson, "The Great Paradox of China: Green Energy and Black Skies," *Environment 360*, August 17, 2009. http:// e360.yale.edu.

Michael A. Levi, "The Party's Over: Why Copenhagen Was the Climate Conference to End All Climate Conferences," *Slate*, December 21, 2009. www.slate.com.

Jim Motavalli, "6 Hot New Electric Cars Soon to Hit Showrooms," *Daily Green*, March 17, 2010. www.thedailygreen .com.

Peter Welch, "Create New Jobs and Save the Planet," *Politico*, March 11, 2010. www.politico.com.

Web Sites

Apollo Alliance (http://apolloalliance.org). A coalition of labor, business, environmental, and community leaders working to encourage a clean-energy revolution and to create high-quality, green-collar jobs.

The Heritage Foundation: Energy and Environment (www .heritage.org/research/energyandenvironment). A conservative think tank's ideas on energy policy and climate change.

Intergovernmental Panel on Climate Change (IPCC) (www .ipcc.ch). An intergovernmental scientific body set up by the United Nations Environment Programme that seeks to provide objective information and reports about climate change science.

Natural Resources Defense Council (www.nrdc.org). This environmental organization's Web site includes a special section on global warming and related issues.

Pew Center on Global Climate Change (www.pewclimate.org). A nonpartisan, science-based organization that provides both basic and in-depth information about all aspects of the climate change issue, including clean-energy technologies and economic aspects.

Pew Research Center (http://pewresearch.org). A nonpartisan "fact tank" that provides information on attitudes about climate change and clean-energy initiatives.

The Sierra Club (www.sierraclub.org/globalwarming). The Sierra Club is a grassroots environmental organization active on global warming and renewable energy issues.

Union of Concerned Scientists (www.ucsusa.org). This science-based organization provides in-depth information and news about global warming and clean energy.

U.S. Environmental Protection Agency—Climate Change (www.epa.gov/climatechange). An informative federal government Web site on the science and effects of—and solutions to—climate change.

Index

About the Author

Debra A. Miller is a writer and lawyer with a passion for current events, history, and public policy. She began her law career in Washington, DC, where she worked on legislative, policy, and legal matters in government, public interest, and private law firm positions. She lives with her husband in Encinitas, California. She has written and edited numerous books, anthologies, and other publications.